"Perfect Omena Day!"

Selections from the Summer Diaries
of Rebecca L. Richmond
1907-1920

Edited by M. Christine Byron
Foreword by Marsha Buehler

Leelanau Press, a Michigan nonprofit publisher of Leelanau County history, art, writers, and authors, was founded by Barbara and Frank Siepker in 2002. Book proceeds fund new books and the Leelanau Press Research Fellowships at Leelanau Historical Museum.

Leelanau Press, 6898 MacFarlane Road, Glen Arbor, Michigan 49636
231-334-4395, siepker@aol.com., LeelanauPress.com

Library of Congress Control Number: 2025935631

ISBN: 978-0-978-5465-2-6

First Edition
Printed in Canada

Dedication

This book is dedicated to those people who have saved various historical documents, including photographs, letters, and diaries and donated them to historical archives, libraries, museums, and other history collections, so that they are preserved for future generations.

Foreword

Christine Byron and I met at Cherry Basket Farm in Omena, a historic farmstead that my husband Tom and I were restoring. Chris kindly brought us a copy of a c.1935 "home movie" of the farm from the Grand Rapids Public Library archives. We were thrilled! We had found no early photos of the farm, and now there was Miss Bailey, waving at us from the farmhouse door as the camera panned around the farmyard.

As we walked around the farm we chatted a bit about the historical connections between Omena and Grand Rapids. Chris had become interested in the diaries of a woman named Rebecca Richmond, owner of an early resort cottage. In a satisfying moment of small-world connection, I told Chris that we knew of Rebecca Richmond because we owned her 1897 cottage! It was exciting to share my acquaintance of Rebecca with someone else who "knew" her.

My introduction to Rebecca Richmond was in 1987 when we purchased from an estate a little old cottage at the dead end of a two track in Omena. The owner had never used the cottage she had inherited forty years before. Neighbors showed us a false wall panel covering what they called a "hidey hole," where boxes of papers and books belonging to the original owner had long been stashed. The trove of musty material took me time-traveling. I spent evenings that summer snooping through Rebecca's correspondence (she kept drafts of her responses as well as the letters received), receipts (some were for items still in the cottage), books and magazines. An impression of Rebecca emerged as an educated, self-assured woman "of a certain age," with means and firm opinions, well respected and generous, having a breadth of interests, experience, and acquaintance.

A chance sighting of a photo in T.J. Stiles' Pulitzer Prize winning *Custer's Trials: A Life on the Frontier of a New America* was stunning: "my" Rebecca was shown with Libbie and George A. Custer at Lincoln's second inauguration.

Rebecca's letters were featured in early programs of the newly organized Omena Historical Society. Amanda Holmes borrowed our cardboard turkey boxes full of letters and ephemera and used the contents in research for her Ph.D. dissertation, and later in her Michigan History Award winning book *Omena: A Place in Time.* published by the OHS in 2003.

Rebecca's papers had become "The Buehler Family Collection," sorted and stored in more respectful fashion than the cardboard turkey boxes, yet the collection languished on the heap of potential projects, intended but not begun.

Meanwhile, in Grand Rapids, Christine Byron had begun her acquaintance with Rebecca Richmond. Chris was the Local Historical Collections librarian for the Grand Rapids Public Library from 2000 until she retired in 2012. In this capacity she learned about Rebecca Richmond's diaries and used one of her diary entries in her first book, *Vintage Views of Leelanau County*, in 2002.

Chris mentally noted that she wanted to do something with RR's diaries. That "something" is *"Perfect Omena Day!" Selections from the Summer Diaries of Rebecca L. Richmond 1907-1920*. Christine Byron's curiosity and generosity have produced a charming and informative book that is chock full of wonderful photographs and postcard images collected over the years. Chris and her husband, Tom Wilson, are active historians. They have an eye for a unique image or brochure and are generous in sharing their finds.

Rebecca Richmond was a person of consequence and influence in her own right, as well as a chronicler of her times. I'm delighted that Chris has included background information from her research about Rebecca and her family in her book.

The simple diary entries chosen and transcribed by Chris for this book are gentle lessons in cultural anthropology blended with a bit of archeology. In a few lines the writer tells of weather, health, worship, and entertainment, social organization and customs, building projects and beautification, and modes of travel and accommodation. We can piece the bits together and know life in the Omena resort of the early 1900s. Many small questions are answered here: when was this wall built and by whom? Where were the rustic structures seen in old photos? How – and with whom - did the cottagers socialize? The history of a small place is personal, full of connections and common ground. Filling in the missing piece of the puzzle, connecting the dots, is a satisfying pastime. Members of my family were early cottagers. My great-grandfather's 1903 cottage is still in our family, so many bits from the past are meaningful and have context to me. We learn that in 1914 Rebecca enjoyed a stay at "The Towers," a home owned by my great-grandfather's brother. The building is now the Omena Historical Society's Putnam-Cloud Tower House Museum.

You will enjoy *Perfect Omena Day!* whether or not you've been to Omena.

Marsha Buehler, Putnam-Cloud Tower House Museum Director

Acknowledgments

First of all, I would like to thank Barbara and Frank Siepker for establishing the Leelanau Press Research Fellowship grant. As the 2024 recipient of the fellowship, I am forever grateful for their generosity and commitment to preserving Leelanau County's history. Rebecca Richmond's Omena summer diaries offer a first-hand account of cottage life in Leelanau County from 1907-1920. These years coincide with the golden age of postcards, and I chose postcards to illustrate many of her diary entries. I am grateful that Leelanau Press had agreed to publish this book so others can share Rebecca's life and times in Omena.

And I would like to thank Rebecca Richmond herself for saving her diaries and ensuring that they were donated to the Grand Rapids Public Library along with other material that she saved for their historical importance. I also want to thank the staff of the Grand Rapids History Center at the Grand Rapids Public Library for their assistance, attention, and support on this project.

My deepest appreciation goes to Marsha Buehler of the Omena Historical Society, who now owns Rebecca Richmond's Omena cottage. Her knowledge and willingness to share the Buehler Family Collection of documents and photographs gave me even more insight to Rebecca's life in Omena. Marsha's agreement to write the foreword to this book, and her encouragement for this project overall means so much to me. The archives of the Omena Historical Society shared many images that related directly to what Rebecca was writing about in her diaries.

For their generous gift of their time, knowledge, and resources, I extend special thanks to the Leelanau Historical Society and Museum for access to their archives and use of historical images from their collection. Kim Kelderhouse, Elizabeth Adams, and Emma Keaton have all been most helpful.

I am grateful to railroad historians Jim Winslow Sr. and Mark Worrall for sharing their knowledge and images of the Grand Rapids & Indiana Railroad.

Many thanks to Julie Christianson Stivers for reading the manuscript, and her skill with the English language and editorial guidance.

With special thanks to Dianne Carroll Burdick for the exquisite hand-coloring of the image on the cover

Much gratitude goes to Rob Burdick for the beautifully rendered design of this book, and for his patience and understanding in dealing with all the details it takes to bring a manuscript into a printed book.

Contents

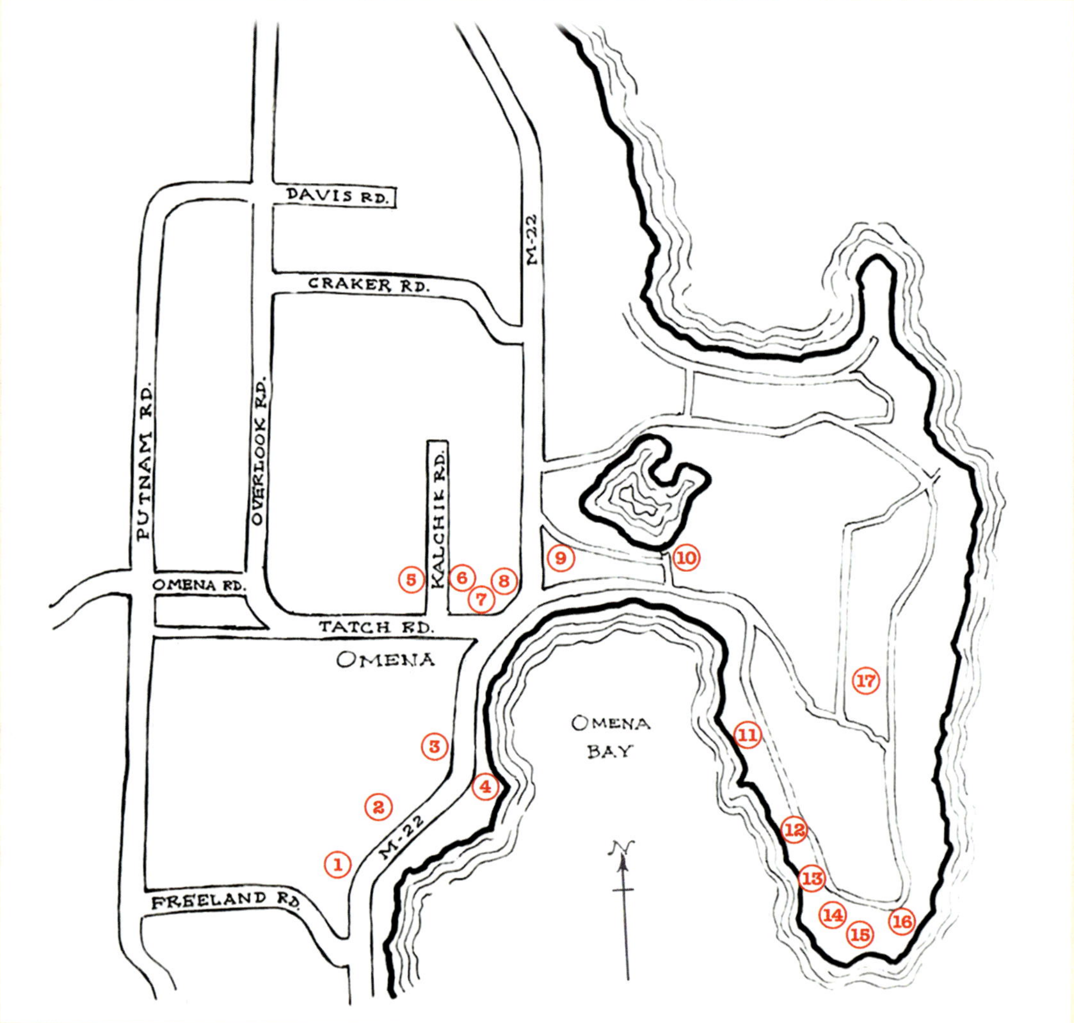

Omena Village and Omena Point

1. Sargent cottage
2. The Clovers
3. The Towers
4. Weaver cottage
5. Train Station
6. Sunset Lodge
7. Anderson Store & Post Office
8. Barth Store
9. Presbyterian Church
10. Congregational Church
11. Pavilion
12. Indian Garden
13. Miss Richmond's cottages: Bonnie Banks & Camp Lookout
14. Oaks Hotel
15. Heart's Ease
16. Grierson, Cutcheon, Pierson, Crabtree, Bevier, Palmer & Chichester cottages
17. Leelanau Hotel

Who Was Rebecca L. Richmond?

Family History:

The Richmond family was one of Grand Rapids' early pioneering families, settling there in the 1830s. Her father, William Almy Richmond, immigrated to Grand Rapids in 1836. He served as a Democratic State Senator at Detroit from 1842-1845 and was a Superintendent of Indian Affairs for Michigan and Wisconsin, 1845-1849. He was responsible for the construction of a power canal and a bridge in Grand Rapids, and later served as President of the Grand Rapids Bridge Co. He was a member of the first board of village trustees, and a cashier at the first bank, the Grand River Bank. He was twice commissioned Brigadier General of the Michigan State Militia. In 1837 he married Loraine Zilpha Page, and they had had three children: Rebecca, Jonathan, and Mary. The family lived with their young children for a number of years in the Sweets Hotel, which served as a sort of family boarding house for some of the city's prominent families. This was a lifestyle Rebecca continued as an adult, boarding at the Morton House and Warwick Hotel for a number of years. She spent the last 15 years or so at the Elmwood, an "apartment hotel" on Cherry St. She never owned a home in Grand Rapids.

William A. Richmond

Loraine Z. Page

Rebecca was cousin of Elizabeth (Libbie) Bacon Custer. Libbie's father was Judge Daniel Bacon and her mother was Eleanor Page Bacon, sister to Rebecca's mother, Loraine Page Richmond. After Libbie's mother died in 1854, Loraine became a kind of surrogate mother to Libbie for a time. Libbie, and sisters Rebecca and Mary Richmond became close as children and stayed in touch throughout their lives. Libbie, when living with her father in Monroe, Michigan, met a young Army officer, George Armstrong Custer, and they married in 1864.

Seated are George Armstrong Custer, and Libbie Bacon Custer. Standing from left to right, Rebecca Richmond, Mary Richmond Kendall and Charles Kendall. circa 1874.

Another prominent cousin of Rebecca Richmond was Frederick Stuart Church. They were second cousins since their grandmothers were sisters. They corresponded frequently and he sometimes sent her drawings from his studio in New York. Rebecca donated some of his work for an exhibit at the Grand Rapids Art Association. She also donated several works of his art to the Grand Rapids Public Library.

Rebecca Richmond's Life in Grand Rapids

Rebecca Loraine Richmond was born on June 22, 1840, the oldest of three children. Her earliest school years were spent at what she called the "little school for girls on Prospect Hill" where she attended classes with other daughters of Grand Rapids pioneers. When she came to "finishing school" age, her parents had the choice of sending her to a convent in Detroit or a seminary out East, since there was no university education for women at that time. So Rebecca attended Brooklyn Heights Seminary in New York, graduating in 1859. She then attended Grand Rapids College in 1861, but the school closed on account of the Civil War.

Rebecca was in her twenties living in Grand Rapids at the time of the Civil War. She recorded daily life and important events in her diaries from 1860-1864. The diaries serve as a historical account of life during that period. She wrote about the day when some of the young men she knew left Grand Rapids as soldiers for the Civil War, and mentioned various battles as news was telegraphed. And she recorded the sad news when local soldiers died in the war, or wounded veterans returned home.

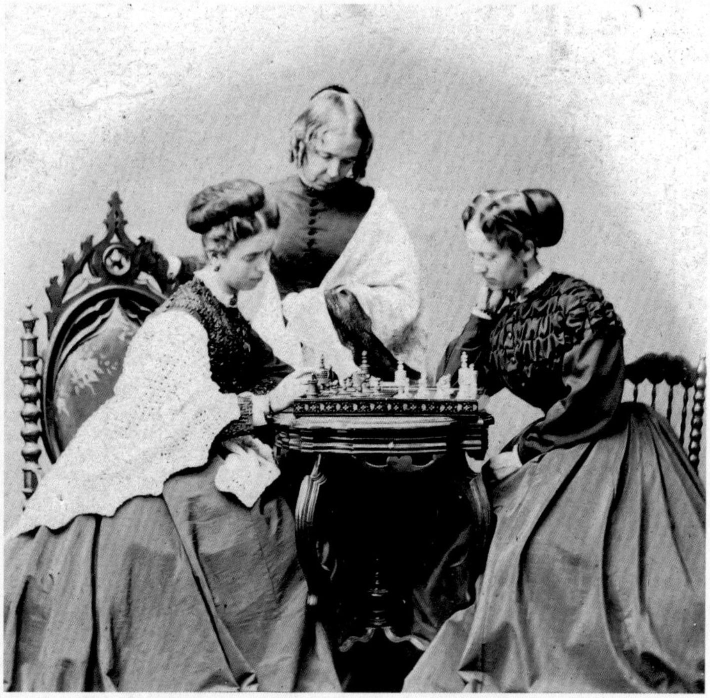

Lorraine Page Richmond (center) with her daughters Rebecca (right) and Mary (left), circa early 1860s

As a young person, Rebecca Richmond had an active social life, attending various events with friends or family, and entertaining in her home. She had a wide range of friends. Throughout her life, either in Grand Rapids, Omena, or traveling, Rebecca enjoyed people's company and companionship. She kept in touch with friends and family and wrote frequent letters, often recording correspondence in her diaries.

The Richmond family were members of St. Mark's Episcopal Church, one of the earliest churches in Grand Rapids. As a young woman she sang in the church choir, taught Sunday School, and became involved with church activities, an allegiance she kept her entire life.

No diaries survive after 1864 until 1907. Rebecca's life in her 30s and 40s is not well documented. But as she grew older, she is mentioned frequently in the *Grand Rapids Press* for her involvement in a variety of causes. She became well-known for her works of charity. After her father died in 1870, she inherited a substantial sum of money, as well as some real estate. She very likely made investments herself and grew her nest egg over the years.

St. Mark's Episcopal Church favored a progressive, social gospel with concern for the poor and Rebecca contributed gifts of $500 to St. Mark's missions. She was appointed in 1886 Vice-President of the St. Mark's Missionary Society.

In 1902 she was elected Secretary, and in 1909, Vice-President of the Woman's Auxiliary of the Protestant Episcopal Diocese of Western Michigan. Rebecca attended conferences in this capacity in various cities in West Michigan and became friends with some of the major figures in the Episcopal Church. She also was a benefactor to other local churches. In 1917 Rebecca gave $500 toward the building fund for St. Phillip's Episcopal Church, the first predominantly African-American church in the Episcopal Western Michigan Diocese.

Rebecca supported the Charity Organization Society of Grand Rapids, the Young Women's Christian Association (YWCA) as well as the Young Men's Christian Association (YMCA). She gave $20,000 to Butterworth Hospital to fund the Rebecca L. Richmond Memorial Room, which offered a free bed to those in need. She also made many smaller gifts throughout the years.

Rebecca was a donor to the Akeley Hall/Institute in Grand Haven, a school for girls associated with the Episcopal Church, for which she endowed the Chair for Domestic Science.

In 1902 she was appointed Secretary of the Grand Rapids and Kent County Humane Society. Then in 1908 through 1911, she was elected as one of the Vice-Presidents of the Michigan Humane Society.

In 1913 Rebecca gave financial aid to the Women's Home Helpers, who in cooperation with the Women's Christian Temperance Union (WCTU), built and operated the Isabella Home for Aged Women on East Fulton in Grand Rapids.

She served on various committees, meeting many of the city's movers and shakers. Her diaries recorded the Christmas cards and gifts she received, some years taking up to three pages. It seemed that she knew all the prominent people of Grand Rapids as evidenced in her diaries, where she recorded some of the social invitations and affairs she attended.

Over the years, Rebecca also gave gifts anonymously, including a $3,000 donation to the District Nursing Association in 1914. Her $10,000 gift to help construct St. Cecilia Music Society's auditorium was intended to be an anonymous gift, but the President of the Society insisted on thanking her publicly because of the size of the gift.

An early view of Richmond Park before amenities were added.

She may be best known in Grand Rapids for her 1915 donation of 10 acres for Richmond Park, which she did to honor her parents. Her gift grew over the next few years to a total of 34 acres. The park now covers about 43 acres featuring open space, woodland, and natural areas. A swimming pool and other amenities make this a popular park for all ages.

Cultural Interests

Rebecca had a passion for music, playing the guitar herself. In her twenties she attended "singing school," and led the children's singing in Sunday School, as well as participating in St. Mark's choir. She was well-informed on the history of music, and often attended lectures on the subject as well as musical performances and concerts. Rebecca funded beautiful stained-glass windows at St. Mark's Church as a tribute to former members of the Church choir. She helped establish a scholarship at the St. Cecilia Music Society in 1915, and often was a patron of other musical enterprises.

Rebecca was a member of the Grand Rapids Art Association (now the Grand Rapids Art Museum) and made several valuable gifts to the institution, including works by her cousin, the eminent artist Frederick Stuart Church. She also gave one of Church's widely known paintings, "Knowledge is Power" to the Grand Rapids Public Library. The painting shows a college girl in a cap and gown and at her feet crouch a group of wild beasts, tamed and overawed. It is on display in the Vander Veen Room of the Grand Rapids Public Library.

Rebecca was very interested in local history and wrote an article, "The Fur Traders of the Grand River Valley," which was originally published in the *Michigan Tradesman* in 1907. She donated various books, ephemera and manuscripts to the Grand Rapids Public Library and was an active member of the Grand Rapids Historical Society. She corresponded regularly with Samuel Ranck, the director of the library and became good friends with Miss Annie Pollard, the assistant librarian, inviting her to stay at her Omena cottage.

Miss Richmond wrote frequent letters to Grand Rapids newspapers concerning topics and events of local interest. For many years, when prominent local persons passed away, Rebecca wrote tributes which were treasured by their families.

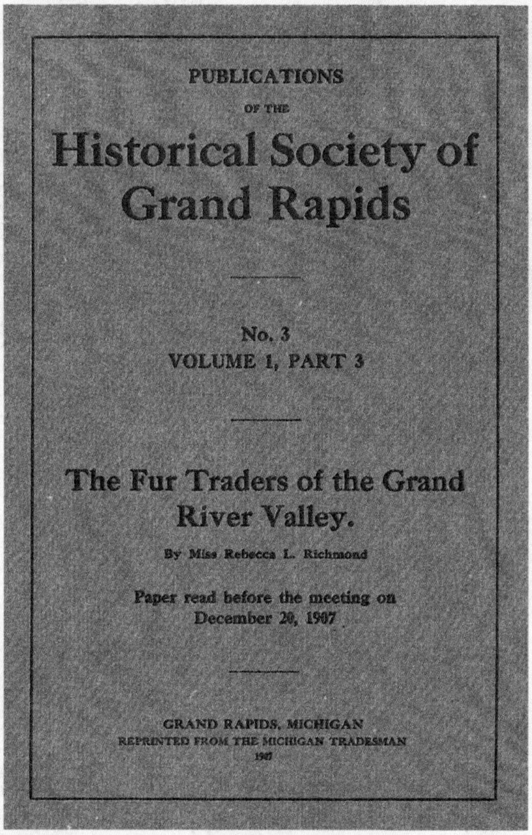
PUBLICATIONS

OF THE

Historical Society of Grand Rapids

No. 3

VOLUME 1, PART 3

The Fur Traders of the Grand River Valley.

By Miss Rebecca L. Richmond

Paper read before the meeting on December 20, 1907

GRAND RAPIDS, MICHIGAN

REPRINTED FROM THE MICHIGAN TRADESMAN

1907

She enjoyed traveling, and visiting her cousin Libbie Custer, wife of General George Armstrong Custer, as well as her sister, Mary Richmond Kendall, and brother, Jonathan Richmond.

She visited the Custers at their headquarters during the Civil War and was one of the "belles of the company" when the staff occupied Senator Mason's home in Virginia in the winter of 1863-64. She attended the dedication of the General George Armstrong Custer monument in Monroe in 1910.

In the time period of her diaries presented in this book, 1907-1920, she made several extended trips. In 1912-13 she spent December through May with her sister Mary in California. In 1914 she traveled to Auburn, New York to visit her aunt, Nancy Eagles. In 1916 she visited Atlanta, as well as other cities over the years.

Rebecca's Life in Omena

Omena is on the west arm of Grand Traverse Bay, about 20 miles north of Traverse City. A narrow tongue of land extends out into the bay, forming a sheltered harbor, Omena Bay. From the beach the land rises in natural terraces to a height of over 100 feet, and cottages were built upon the terraces.

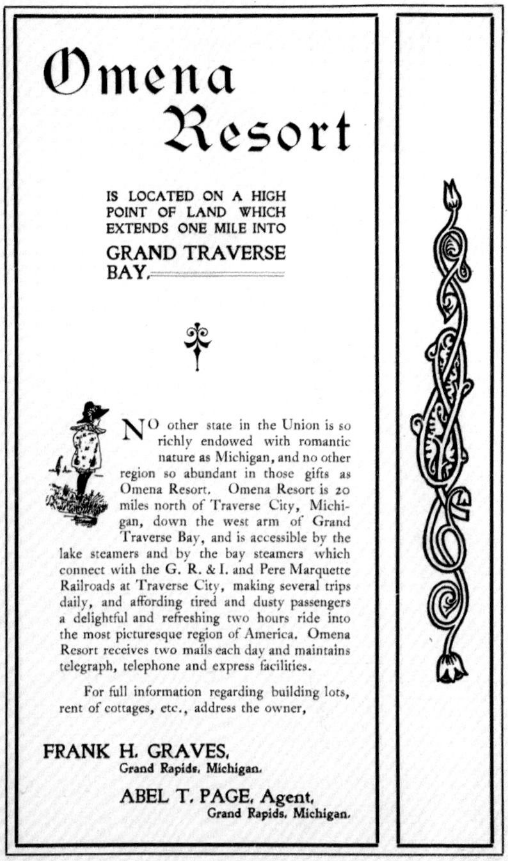

Rebecca became familiar with Omena from her uncle, Abel T. Page, an insurance agent and real estate agent in Grand Rapids. He partnered with Frank Graves, another Grand Rapidian, to plan and market Omena Bay Resort. The plan for the resort was for cottages to be built that would make central use of the nearby hotels, the Oaks and the Omena Inn, for meals and social gatherings. It was common in those days for cottages to be built without kitchens.

We know she visited the area, at least as early as 1891, because an article from the *Grand Rapids Herald* states that Miss Richmond and her mother spent the summer of 1891 at the "Grand Traverse Bay resorts."

Rebecca must have loved the area. In 1896, she purchased waterfront property for a cottage. Other lots that year were bought by Eleanor Willard, William Weed, and Ellen B. Currier. In the following years Clara D. Pierson, Ellen Dean, John Moore, John Santo, Mary and Cornelia Bevier, Mary A. Spear, the Roods, the McCutcheons, the Stevens, and the Griersons also purchased property and built cottages on Omena Point. Rebecca's cottage, "Bonnie Banks" was built in 1897. Rebecca acquired her second cottage, "Camp Lookout," from her neighbors in 1908. She often rented the cottages or let friends use them at no charge. She led a busy social life and had a wide circle of friends, both local and summer residents. Together they enjoyed the simple pleasures of cottage life, including dinner at local hotels, evenings on the piazza, or leisurely strolls through the woodlands.

Transportation to Omena

When Rebecca first started coming to Omena, she would have taken either the Grand Rapids & Indiana Railway or the Pere Marquette Railway to Traverse City, and then taken a steamer to Omena. Some of the boats that regularly traveled on Grand Traverse Bay and docked at Omena included the "S.S. Missouri," "S.S. Puritan" and the "S.S. Manitou" of the Northern Michigan Transportation Company. A smaller boat, the "Chequamegon," of the Traverse Bay Transportation Company, began service in 1907. Since Rebecca's diaries from the period start with 1907, it would not have been necessary for her to take a boat from Traverse City to Omena since the railroad came to Omena in 1903.

The Traverse City Leelanau & Manistique Railroad (TCL &M), operated by the Grand Rapids & Indiana Railway (GR & I), started service to Northport in 1903, with stops at Bingham, Suttons Bay and Omena. The GR & I attempted to boost its declining revenue by establishing a cross-lake ferry to Manistique from Northport, but that failed to produce enough revenue to sustain the route.

The train schedule varied over the years, but at least one passenger train stopped in Omena daily except Sunday. Rebecca frequently took the GR & I from Grand Rapids to Traverse City, stayed a night or two at the Park Place Hotel, and continued via rail to Omena on the next day. The first depot at Omena was a boxcar. Later, in 1916, a station was built. The train also made stops at the Clovers Hotel.

Death in 1925

Upon Rebecca's death in 1925, her cottage, Bonnie Banks, was passed on to her dear friend, Miss Edna Spillard.

Rebecca left $6,000 to St. Mark's, including funds for a choir endowment, missionary work, and Camp Roger, a West Michigan Christian Day Camp for children. She left a trust fund of $61,000 to the Isabella Home for Aged Women.

In her will, Miss Richmond left $5,000 to the Grand Rapids Public Library, which was to be used for the purchase of books related to landscape gardening, in which she was greatly interested. She donated the family papers, photographs, and ephemera to the Grand Rapids History Center of the Grand Rapids Public Library. The Richmond Family Papers Collection include some family history, Rebecca's diaries, and her autograph books, which contain signatures of General George Armstrong Custer and Mark Twain. She left $2,000 to the Grand Rapids Historical Society, which was to be used for funding lectures, the first of which was presented in 1927. $2,000 was bequeathed to the Grand Rapids Welfare Union.

Rebecca was a benefactor to hospitals, educational institutions, churches, clubs, and to individuals in need. *The Grand Rapids Press* wrote in her obituary, "In a quiet, unostentatious way she went about doing good."

Rebecca Richmond's diaries that have survived cover the Civil War years 1860 -1864, and then the years 1907-1920, which is the period that this book covers. Like many diarists, Rebecca did not write everyday. In 1909 there were no entries for the summer months, and in 1912, only one summer entry was found. While the entire content of her diaries gives interesting background to her life in Grand Rapids, the focus of this book is on Rebecca's time spent in Omena, which was predominantly during the summer months. The selection from her diaries which follow were mostly chosen for their content relating to Omena. Some entries only included information of letters she received or sent, and were not included, because they did not add much to the overview of Rebecca's life in Omena. I have kept the spellings, punctuation, abbreviations, and other idiosyncrasies that Ms. Richmond used in her diaries. Because the time period of 1907-1920 was during the golden age of postcards, many references that Rebecca made could be illustrated with postcards. Other photos and ephemera were chosen for their similar relevance. Although she would not have known it at the time, her portrait of cottage life at Omena gives today's reader a glimpse back to a quieter, gentler time.

The Grand Rapids Public Library holds Rebecca Richmond's diaries in the Richmond Family Collection.

"Perfect Omena Day!"
Selections from the Summer Diaries of Rebecca L. Richmond, 1907-1920

1907

Tues., June 11, 1907
Bright & mild. Started at 2:20 for Omena: dustless, pleasant trip, arr. Trav. C. at 7:30.

Wed., June 12, 1907
Delightful! Tripped about on errands, Co. store [Hannah & Lay Mercantile] on a/c of pump, etc. Dined with Mrs. Barnes and two other ladies at Park [Place] Hotel. ... Left at 3:40 on mixed train & arr. at Omena & Sunset Lodge at 5:40. Mr. & Mrs. Wheeler welcomed me. ... [Wheelers owned the Sunset Lodge]

Thurs., June 13, 1907
Fine! Car ferry excursion to Old Mission; all the villagers gone. Mr. & Mrs. Geo. Agosa carried Alida Jacobson & me to The Point, and Andrew spent morning helping at my cottage. We opened other 2 & found everything in order. Lunched by myself and walked home alone.

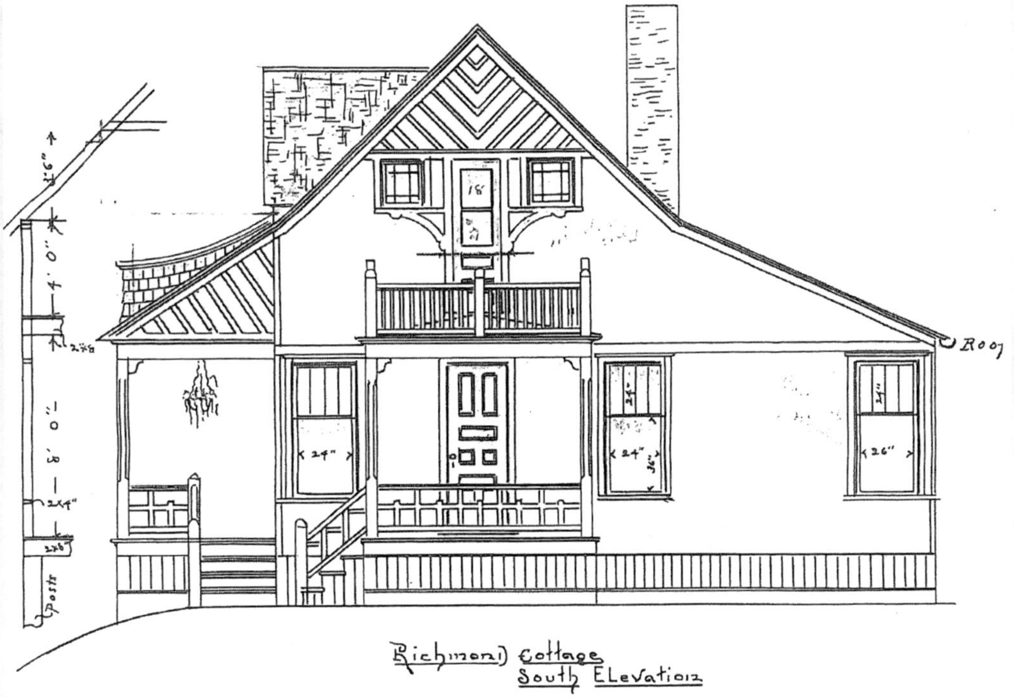

Rebecca Richmond's cottage, Bonnie Banks, built in 1897
Architectural drawing of south elevation.

Fri., June 14, 1907
Fine. Walked out to cottage & rode back with Noekels who came to depot to meet Miss Barr & her niece who came from Jacksonville to the Oaks. Lunched at Mrs. Bradley's...

Sat., June 15, 1907
Fine, but pretty hot. Andrew spent 3/4 day at my cottage: all in readiness for occupancy outside & in. Walked both ways and very tired tonight. Mr. Ed. Rood & wife called and inspected cottage. They have been spending two weeks honeymoon at the father's cottage, Sunnyside.

Sun., June 16, 1907
Breezey & hot. Attended church with Mr. & Mrs. Wheeler & guests. ... At 4 o'cl went to Indian Ch. [Omena Presbyterian Church]: about 30 present, very devout. 3 Agosa men & families present, sons of last chief.

Mon., June 17, 1907
Hot. Left "Sunset Terrace" for Bonnie Banks by omnibus: pd. for 5 days $5 & gave $10 to ch. Mrs. Monroe came at 5:20 and we took supper at "The Oaks" with Miss Barr & niece & friend... Pd. for carrying furniture $1.50 & 2 pas. [passengers] & trunk $1.00.

OLD INDIAN MISSION CHURCH, OMENA, MICH.

1908

Fri., July 3, 1908
Mr. Hunt escorted me to 7:00 am train for Omena: Mrs. Wilkinson of Ionia joined me at Howard City. Great crowd fr. Walton to Traverse where they have 2 day celebration. Omena, at Wheeler's for supper & night. Very cool.

Sat., July 4, 1908
Nice ride to "Bonnie Banks" this morn., fire quickly lighted & cottage regulated; all cleaned.

Sun., July 5, 1908
Warm. Steady rain all morn: held up awhile this afternoon. We had vesper service on piazza [porch], 49th Ps. etc. Rain again tonight.

Mon., July 6, 1908
Rained so hard we could not go to breakfast: woman brot [brought] 1 quart milk. Busy afternoon at Camp Lookout [Rebecca's second cottage].

Tues., July 7, 1908
48 degrees this morn. Rain ceased at noon & at 1 o'cl. Mr. Hunter and his men began work on my frontage, cement walk. Finished Camp Lookout cleaning this morn & this afternoon Mr. Moffat took lower sleeping room.

Rustic Gateway near Indian Garden

Wed., July 8, 1908
Had lovely eve. at Mrs. Santo's with music.

Thurs., July 9, 1908
Delightful! Hunter completed grading & filling. Gravel added to my upper road & path. We helped Mrs. Blair this eve. celebrate the 25th anniversary of Rev. Bradley's marriage.

Fri., July 10, 1908
High wind & waves. Retaining wall completed on beach. Saw the sunset from cement sofa on beach, foot of Forest Ave. Sang in hammock by moonlight till 10 o'cl. Called on Mrs. Graves & Mrs. Pound. Visited Indian Garden.

Sun., July 12, 1908
Lovely day. Mrs. Wilkinson, Mr. Moffat & I had morning service on my piazza, 49th Ps., several hymns etc. He sings a fine tenor.

Mon., July 13, 1908
This eve Mr. & Mrs. Pound & Martha & her friend Dorothy sang on our piazza.

Thurs., July 16, 1908
Mrs. W. [Wilkerson] & I went to Traverse C. by afternoon train; fr. 4:20 to 6 did the town, saw "The Toiler" at Co. Store [Hannah & Lay Mercantile] etc. Gov. Warner & Lt. Gov. Kelly at supper & and band in front of hotel. Rain in night.

Fri., July 17, 1908
Rain all afternoon. Mrs. W. went out to Ionia at 6 a.m. I wrote letters for an hour this afternoon, more rain tonight. Miss Susan Yerkes & Grace Diamond came at 6.

Sat., July 18, 1908
Seeing the town with the friends this morn. I took 3 p.m. train for Omena: supper at Wheelers & night. More rain. Nice people here.

Sun., July 19, 1908
Pleasant. On the morn train came Miss Yerkes & Miss Grace D. [Diamond]. Mr. Wheeler's carriage took us out to cottage: after dinner at the Oaks walked along the terrace to Cherokee [Lodge]. Eve. on piazza with several.

Cherokee Lodge, Omena, Mich.

Mon., July 20, 1908
Pleasant. Miss Yerkes etc. took boat at 10 for Charlevoix & Petoskey. Mrs.Cutcheon spent forenoon with me. ...

Wed., July 22, 1908 Miss Helen Wilkinson, aged 14, arrived from Ionia today to spend 2 weeks with me.

Thurs., July 23, 1908
Mr. & Miss Ayars & Mr. Pence of Crawfordsville, Ind. arr. by "Str. Missouri" this afternoon, have taken 3 rooms at Camp Lookout.

Fri., July 24, 1908
Indian Pow-wow tonight at Cherokee Lodge, invitation by Katherine Chichester. ... Bonfire, Indian dance, etc., etc.

Sun., July 26, 1908
Song service this eve. at Rev. Mr. Bradley's.

Mon., July 27, 1908
This afternoon came man to paint "Camp Lookout." Awful heat in the cities; bad enough here. 83 degrees.

"S.S. Missouri"
Northern Michigan Transportation Co.

Thurs., July 30, 1908
Hot, but breeze part of day. Andrew overcome by heat. Mr. Pence pd. one week's room rent $2.00

Fri., July 31, 1908
In bed, result of heat & working. Helen brings my meals. Wrote Cousin Mary [Richmond] & [Sister] Mary Kendall.

Sat., Aug. 1, 1908
Mrs. MacBride & Josephine arrived on afternoon train. Mr. Hunter has finished my cement walk & the painting of Camp Lookout.

Sun., Aug. 2, 1908
Song service tonight by Rev. Hartley. Wrote Mary R. to meet me at Traverse City.

Mon., Aug. 3, 1908
Mr. & Mrs. Burchard, Howard, Ellen & her dog Teddy arrived this afternoon & took rooms at Camp Lookout.

Wed., Aug. 5, 1908
Helen left "Bonnie Banks" this morn. to spend a week with Martha Pound & K. [Kate] Chichester. At 6 o'cl, I took boat for Traverse, nice moonlight ride, arr. 8:30 at Park [Place] Hotel. Found letter from Cous. Mary.

Moonlight on Grand Traverse Bay

Thurs., Aug. 6, 1908 - Traverse City
Moved this afternoon to Mrs. Parker's, [Julia Parker] State St. Cous. Mary & Chas. Richmond arrived at 6 pm fr. A. Arbor to spend a week with me: they at Park Hotel.

Fri., Aug. 7, 1908
Spent morning showing the cousins about town. Cool & cloudy & breezy: wool suits.

Sat., Aug. 8, 1908
Very cool night & morn. Long drive about city this afternoon.

Sun., Aug 9, 1908
Very cool morn; fine rest of day. We three attended Grace Ch. this morn. Fine sermon by Rev. Atwill & good music. Met Aux. [Woman's Auxiliary of the Protestant Episcopal Diocese of Western Michigan] after service.

Wed., Aug. 12, 1908
Train for Omena at 9:30 am. Pd. my room rent, $2.50 and their hotel bill $20.00 [presumably the cousins' bill at the Park Hotel]. ...

Thurs., Aug. 13, 1908
Cousins Charles & Mary delighted with Omena Point & with "Bonnie Banks."

Sun., Aug. 16, 1908
Pretty hot & sultry. Very hot in G.R. Mr. Howard returned to G. Rapids, having been at Camp Lookout 2 wk. [weeks] I give them all free use of rooms, 3.

Mon., Aug. 17, 1908
Morning drive with Mrs. Howard, Mary & I. This afternoon at my house a dozen listened to Mr. Ayars talk about the 36 birds he has observed here since July 23.

Tues., Aug. 18, 1908
Picnic by launch to Gull Island, Chas. went. Very high wind & waves. Wrote letter for "Record-Herald" of Traverse. Pd. for W.B. Willard's cement walk & sent him rec't.

Wed., Aug. 19, 1908
Wrote Gifford Pinchot, Forestry Dept. about Omena Point.

Thurs., Aug. 20, 1908
High wind. Chas. did repairs on stairway to the beach; M. [Mary] & I helped with graveling paths. On the Chi. [Chicago] boat this eve. went Mr. & Mrs. Ayars & Capt. Pence of Camp Lookout. Ayars & Pence pd. in full for rooms at Camp Lookout. We spent eve. reading aloud "Capt. Eri" a Cape Cod story.

"S.S. Manitou"
Northern Michigan Transportation Co.
Service ran from Chicago to Mackinac Island with ports of call including Traverse City, Suttons Bay, Omena, & Northport

Sat., Aug. 22, 1908
Mrs. Howard and Ellen & Josephine MacBride returned to G. Rapids this afternoon after 3 weeks at Camp Lookout by courtesy.

Sun., Aug. 23, 1908
Mary & Charles went to village this afternoon to Cong. Ch. ... This eve. Chas. & I went to Song Service at Bradley's, Rev Hartley leading.

Mon., Aug. 24, 1908
Pleasant. Cousins M [Mary] & C [Charles] went to Charlevoix on the "Chequamegon," returning at evening. Saw the Stanleys & Prices.

"S.S. Chequamegon"
Traverse Bay Transportation Company

Tues., Aug. 25, 1908
Mary & I walked over to Mr. Wheeler's for tea & went to a fine concert at Cong. Ch. by Fisk Male Quartette: rode home. [Pd.] to Geo. Sands for team & driver 2 days on road hauling clay $6.00. [Pd.] A. P. Hunter, painting "Camp Lookout," check $45.00.

Fisk University Jubilee Male Quartette, from left: Alfred G.King (first bass), James A. Myers (second tenor), Noah W. Ryder (second bass), and John W. Work II first tenor)

Thurs., Aug. 27, 1908
Hazy & cool morn, warmer at eve. Cous. Mary Richmond left for home at 8:20 after 3 weeks visit with me. She is to stop overnight at Bp. Gillespie's. Wrote this eve, to Cous. Mary Church & to Sister Mary Kendall. Rec'd of Mrs. Blair $12 in full for Moffat's rooms to Sept. 8.

Fri., Aug. 28, 1908
Hazy, breezy & showers. Chas. & I did a lot of regulating this morn.

Sun., Aug. 30, 1908
Pd. by check on Traverse C. State Bank, to A.P. Hunter, balance on cement walk, $70.50.

Mon., Sept. 7, 1908
Went down to Traverse this afternoon in company with the Bevier sisters [Nell & Mary]. ... Mrs. Bailey, Pres. of Aux. met me & had conference in the absence of Rev. Atwill & wife.

Tues., Sept. 8, 1908
Met Mrs. F. Lyon at Park Hotel & invited her to go to Omena; she will go Thurs.

Santo's home

Wed., Sept. 9, 1908
Got home this morn. & found Mr. Hunter & Cous. Chas. had nearly enclosed the portico over front door. Pd. Hunter for work enclosing portico. $50.00

Thurs., Sept. 10, 1908
Carrie Lyon arrv'd at 11, Chas. meeting her at station with carriage & giving her quite a ride. Workmen stopped till Monday.

Fri., Sept. 11, 1908
Charles rowed Carrie & me fr. the Oaks down to Santo's this morning.

Sat., Sept. 12, 1908
Mrs. Lyon returned to Traverse this afternoon; we both enjoyed the visit.

Thurs., Sept. 17, 1908
Closed Bonnie Banks at noon & Mr. Wheeler drove Cous. Chas and me to his house to dinner, then took train to Trav. C. with Mrs. Pierson & Miss. Heston. ... Pd. Miss Barr in full to date for board for myself & guests.

Fri., Sept. 18, 1908
The Oaks & The Garrison closed & all hands sailed on the "Missouri" this pm. for Chicago. ... The Hartleys left The Wigwam & The Point is deserted.

Tues., Sept. 22, 1908
Lightning & thunder at 5 a.m. but no rain. Navigation stopped on the St. Lawrence & at The Soo. Fires all over Ontario & northern N.Y. & in our state.

Wed., Sept. 23, 1908
Cooler; light breezes blowing the smoke away from The Point at noon. Mr. Wheeler drove 3 of us out to the cottage. Saw Andrew & gave him directions. Telephoned plumber Barnes.

Passenger steamers, including the "S.S. Missouri" and the "S.S. Manitou," regularly docked at Omena

Thurs., Sept. 24, 1908
Hot & still at noon; heavy pall of smoke hiding the Bay; thunder & a few sprinkles of rain. ... Busy writing.

Fri., Sept. 25, 1908
I have a severe bronchial cold & must go where I can easily consult a doctor. Pd. Mrs. Wheeler for my 9 days & Chas. & my transportation & drivers. $10.00.

Sat., Sept. 26, 1908
Hot & smoky still. Left the Wheelers at 3 pm for Traverse C. where I did some shopping & then Park Hotel. ... Few tourists, season over...

Northwestern Michigan Fair at Traverse City

Fri., Oct. 2, 1908
Clear, crisp, sunny day. The great Northwestern Fair has closed schools & shops & makes struggle to save itself. Lay family have come fr. Chicago. ...

Sat., Oct. 3, 1908
Walked out twice: had Rev & Mrs. Atwill to dinner. Warmer.

Mon., Oct. 5, 1908
Pleasant ride down to G. Rapids. Taking rooms at the Livingston.

1909

No summer diary entries for 1909.

1910

Mon., July 4, 1910
Gloriously cool & bright. Packing this morn. for Omena. ...

Wed., July 6, 1910
... I decided to wait until tomorrow morn. Sister Mary came unexpectedly at 6 this eve: I having rec'd a wire fr. her fr. Chi, waited till she should arrive.

Thurs., July 7, 1910
Cool night, fine sleep for both. Left at 2:10 for Trav. City, arr. at Park Hotel. ...

Sun., July 10, 1910
The Rev. Musson of Moline, Ill. conducted a short morn. service at Bonnie Banks: 15 present...

Mon., July 11, 1910
Lucy Hughes, Lizzie Marsh, Frances H. & her friend Miss Washburn of Belding came on the morn. train to occupy Camp Lookout by courtesy thru the month.

Fri., July 15, 1910
I began to take breakfast at Camp Lookout with one of my guests, the others going to The Oaks. I share costs. Lucy has cottage free for July.

Sun., July 17, 1910
Pleasant. Morn. Service at Bonnie Banks, two officiating clergy, Messrs. Musson & Sulger.

Tues., July 19, 1910
A perfect day, Omena's best. Sister Mary [Kendall] & Emma Earle came fr. Traverse on the morn. train & returned on the 3 p.m. tr. - nice visit. M. much pleased with improvements in 6 years: E. delighted.

Santo's boat house, the "Joy Parlor"

Wed., July 20, 1910
High winds & threatening rain, but picnic party came fr. Traverse C. to Mr. Santos's & Lucy Hughes & I helped serve the 60 children whom a half dz. ladies escorted by boat.

Sun., July 24, 1910
Breezy with fine surf. Morn service in Mr. Santo's "Joy Parlor" over his boat house. Rev. Mr. Musson officiating: 25 present & most impressive.

Tues., July 26, 1910
Showery. Emma Earle who has been visiting Sister M. [Mary] at Park Hotel, Traverse C, the past 10 days, came to Bonnie Banks by this morn's train.

Sat., July 30, 1910
Pleasant. Breakfast at "Camp Lookout." After which Elizabeth & Mary Wilkinson took train for Ionia where they will put home in order for parents. At 3 this afternoon Lucy & Lizzie & Frances & Miss Washburn left Camp Lookout for G.R. Pd. Miss Barr to date for W's & me & settled for breakfast.

Sun., July 31, 1910
Delightful day! Still & warm & partly overcast. Emma E. & I got our breakfast at Camp L. At 11:00 o'cl. Rev. Mr. Sulger held service in my "Sky Parlor" [porch]. 20 persons being present, including Mrs. Cutcheon, Mr. & Mrs. Renwick & Miss Ring & 2 cousins who have not attended before. Rev. Musson & family went by boat yesterday.

Mon., Aug. 1, 1910
Pleasant. Sister Mary came fr. Traverse City on the morn. train: She in Green room, E. Earle in bird room.

Wed., Aug. 3, 1910
Fine rain from early morn. to 5 p.m. Nice breakfast at Camp L, M. had lunch at Bonnie B. & she & E. [Emma] went to tea. Bright fire this eve. & we played Bezique [similar to Pinochle].

Fri., Aug. 5, 1910 - Traverse City
Cool & windy. Early breakfast at Camp Lookout, then Emma E. took train (8:30) for G. Rapids. Then M. & I packed & closed house & Mr. Wheeler took us to the 3 o'clk train for Traverse and Park Hotel. Music at the dinner hour & all bright & pleasant.

Mary Kendall, Rebecca's sister, on the porch of Bonnie Banks

Sat., Aug. 6, 1910 - Traverse City
Cool & bright; fine day for the circus & the "Buster Brown Boots" ad [advertising] him, & his mother & Tige [his dog]. M. & I shopped & visited the Bank & the Santos offices. ... Rev. Mrs. Atwill called this eve.

Sun., Aug. 7, 1910
Cool & grey. M. & I attended Grace Church. 50 people present. Rev. Atwill officiated, assisted by Rev. Stout, visiting, who preached. He and his wife called on us later.

Tues., Aug. 9, 1910 - Trav. City & Omena
Fine rain last night. I off for Omena at 10 a.m. & Mary for G. Rapids at 11: she goes to my rooms at Elmwood. I paid her fare fr. Omena & the hotel bill at Trav, so she has made me a good week's visit; Mr. Remwick & family gone, much to our regret. Cement walk nearly done.

Wed., Aug. 10, 1910
Found a great quantity of mail awaiting me, I am writing. Mrs. MacBride spent eve. here; is to stay nights thro week.

Fri., Aug. 12, 1910
Pleasant. Maj. MacBride arrives this morn to act as 1st mate to Capt. Howard of the "Nancy Ann". This afternoon I cheered Nell Bevier by inviting her to hear letters fr. the Torreys & Mrs. Brown, read from her musical daughter. Singing on Howard's piazza this eve.

Sat., Aug. 13, 1910
Mild & grey. Busy making renovations at Camp Lookout. This eve. entertained the crew of the raft "Nancy Ann"on my illuminated porch & gave prizes: then songs till 10.

Sun., Aug. 14, 1910
Grey & threatening, but quiet & mild. Service on my porch @10:30; Rev. Sulger officiates, 15 present, offer. $2.65. Letter from Bp. [Bishop] McCormick saying he would like to be here Aug 28 for eve. service. ...

Mon., Aug. 15, 1910
... Sister Mary left here at 5:30 yesterday, arr. at Ann Arbor at 9:30. Delia Hazeltine arr this afternoon fr. Charlevoix to visit Ellen Howard at Camp Lookout.

Thurs., Aug. 18, 1910
Cool & breezy. Andrew & I enlarged the seating capacity of the Sky Parlor, [porch] 2 benches, & built platform & table, the last covered with birch bark. Mr. Howard & Ellen, Delia Hazeltine & Josephine MacBride spent the afternoon there in hammocks. ...

Sun., Aug. 21, 1910
Pleasant: warm & quiet. Rev. Mr. Sulger held service at 1 o'cl. in the sky parlor. 15 present. The offering for 3 Sundays has amt. to over $6 for Bp. McCormick's diocesan work...

Sat., Aug. 27, 1910
Mrs. Wilkinson arrived on the afternoon train having made Aux. visits at Thompsonville. ... etc., etc. Very pretty Kodak views of Omena sent by Rev. Musson.

Pere Marquette Depot, Thompsonville, Mich.

Sun., Aug. 28, 1910
Fine. Rev. Sargent brot [brought] Bp. McC., fr. Northport in launch to the Pres. Ch. and Mr. Sargent Jr. assisted in service, Frank Anderson leading singing on piano & Geo. being usher. Ch. full; $12 offering for missions divided. ... Eve. by my firelight with Chinese lanterns. Supper at Oaks...

Mon., Aug. 29, 1910
Such a delightsome morning! A marine treat by the Rev. Sargent & sons of "The Clovers." They are of Indianapolis & Battle C. The launch "Lady Jane" took Bp. McC, Mrs. W. [Wilkinson], Misses Ellen & Joe & Mrs. Sargent Jr., husband & brother-in-law & me on a rollicking trip around the Bay. Eve. at Howards partly, then bezique & music by my fire, Nell Bevier went home today.

Tues., Aug. 30, 1910
Disagreeable! Damp, blowy, showery. After break. Mrs. Howard, Wilkinson & I escorted Bp. McC. to "Heart's Ease," then Rev. Sulger called & his wife & Ellen & Joe took him to Singing Sands. ... Mr. Wheeler called: he had to lose Mrs. Palmer's violin recital on a/c of rain.

The Clovers

Wed., Aug. 31, 1910
Pleasant but cool. The Rev. Sargent family left their bungalow at the Clovers for home today. Mrs. Sulger & her mother Mrs. Alden called this afternoon. ... I am so busy and tired trying to pack up all by myself.

Thurs., Sept. 1, 1910
Mrs. King & Miss Allen closed their cottage & departed today. I called at the Sulgers before tea and left souvenirs for the children.

Sat., Sept. 3, 1910
Andrew spent morn. taking in awnings & other heavy things. I am packing in earnest. Mr. Howard arrived this morn. & they are packing.

Sun., Sept. 4, 1910
Cool & breezy. Spent day pretty much in writing & reading. Mrs. Grierson & Mrs. Cavendar made me a good visit, very informal, but comforting. ... Geo. Anderson called & I gave him civic imp. [improvement] literature & music for his brother.

Mon., Sept. 5, 1910
Rain. Miserable wet morn. to go to breakfast. Had fire & spent some time writing: Pd. Miss Barr chk. for $20 in full. Off for G.R. at 2:40 with Mr. & Mrs. Howard & Ellen & Joshephine MacBride: arr. at 8:30, Miss E.L.C. [Emma L. Chamberlain] waiting for me.

Union Station in Grand Rapids

1911

Thurs., May 4, 1911 - Traverse City
Warmer & sunny. Started for Omena at 3 p.m., pretty run & arrived at 9, at Park Hotel. Mr. & Mrs. Holden & Parsons greeted me. ...

Fri., May 5, 1911 -Omena
Spent forenoon visiting bank & Co. Store, & writing to Sister Mary & Emma C. [Chamberlain] At 2 p.m. came Mrs. Wilkinson fr. Ionia & we took the 4 o'cl train for Omena where Mr. Wilkinson & Wheeler & Carl Swanson met us at station & Mrs. Wheeler at the door.

Sat., May 6, 1911
Fine. After breakfast Mr. Wheeler drove us over to the Point & brought us back at 5:30 for supper. Found Mr. Wilkinson & Carl had put grounds & Camp Lookout into neat order, & we arranged things for M. & Mrs. [Wilkinson] to sleep at Camp L., I at Wheeler's "Sunset Lodge."

Sun., May 7, 1911
Such comfortable accommodations! Nice bed & table, furnace & hearth fire. Quiet morning reading. Wilkinsons walked over to dinner at 12:30. All went to Cong. Ch. together at 3 p.m., then Mr. W [Wheeler] took the W's [Wilkinsons] to drive & I called on Andrew's widow & Mrs. Barth & Mrs. Anderson

Hepatica, commly known as liverleaf or liverwort

Mon., May 8, 1911
Fine. Bright & calm & mild. Breakfast at 7, & Mr. W. & I reached Camp Lookout before they [Wilkinsons] were thru breakfast. My hepatica bed in fine bloom. Prepared another & planted 50 roses & trimmed hedges & trees. Planted beech tree in front.

Tues., May 9, 1911
Morning fog. Walked over this morn, inspected the new pavilion, & found Carl & Mr. W. clearing my 2nd terrace. Squirrel visited us on our evergreen trimmed porch.

Wed., May 10, 1911
Hot & dry. Blazed a trail fr. Woodland Way, back of Bonnie B. [Banks] over to Leelanau Ave. & this afternoon we three went thru it to "Heart's Ease." Closed cottages and rode home with Mr. Wheeler at 5. ...

Thurs., May 11, 1911
Wind. Mr. & Mrs. Wilkinson went home today having had a refeshing time. I devoted myself at Mr. Wheeler's to settling accounts & distributing things. ...

Fri., May 12, 1911
Wind. 8 o'cl train for G.R., Rev. Mr. Bradley company to Traverse & Mr. Hughton [spelling?] from Walton to G.R. Ar. 5 p.m., welcome fr. E.L.C. ...

Thurs., June 29, 1911
Hope to start for Omena.

Wed., July 12, 1911
My guests and I rode over to "The Clovers" & called at the Sargent bungalow. Dr. & Mrs. S. have known Miss Yerkes many years.

Thurs., July 13, 1911
Miss Yerkes left on the 1:30. Elizabeth Wilkinson is detained by an invalid guest, so Miss Lizzie Marsh is to be my guest for the present.

Thurs., Aug 3, 1911
Quite an entertaining Vaudeville at the Pavilion this eve. conducted by the young people.

Sun., Aug 6, 1911
Rev. Mr. Bradley conducted the Song Service tonight in a most pleasing way: charged us to go home and make it easy for others to get such an outing.

Wed., Aug 9, 1911
Left Omena at 1:30, nice cool ride in showers to Cadillac, supper & G. Rapids at 8:30. Mrs. Judge Whithey, reading as usual, with door hospitably open, was the one to welcome me. Rooms nicely cleaned: seems good to be here.

The Omena Pavilion (now Omena-Traverse Yacht Club)

Wed., Aug 30, 1911
Genr'l. B.H. Grierson is dead at "The Garrison," Omena, aged 86.

Thurs., Oct 19, 1911
Started for Omena at 2:40 p.m. accom. by K. [Kate] Earle. Engine gave out at Big Rapids & we were one-and- a-half hrs late at Traverse City, 10 o'cl, Park Place Hotel. ...

Fri., Oct 20, 1911 - Omena, Sunset Lodge
Pleasant. No train on alternate days in the morn. for Omena, so we breakfasted & dined at Park Hotel, called at the Bank, Co. Store, Library, Park, etc. Again at 4 o'cl the engine was off the track. I telephoned Omena and we finally started at quarter to 6. At 7:15 Mr. Wheeler met us at station with lantern & welcome.

Sat., Oct 21, 1911
Pleasant. We had such a good day on The Point. Fire in both cottages: did considerable work, then walked to Cherokee Cottage in the sunshine. Lunch at Bonnie Banks: called on Santos, building new cottages: then rode home with Mr. W.

Sun., Oct 22, 1911
Rain. All day in the house, resting, reading, writing ... Mr. Wheeler & I gave a concert this eve. Singing the book through, "Herrick's Col. of Old songs."

Mon., Oct 23, 1911
Rain all day: no going to the cottage. Wrote to Sister Mary & Emma C. ...

Tues., Oct 24, 1911
Cold & windy. We drove to cottage & spent full day, Mr. Krohn helping this morn. Water-pipes taken up & new plans for pump another year.

Thurs., Oct 26, 1911
Cold & grey. Mr. W. took us to cottage, there meeting with the new caretaker, Mr. Ed Deview who planted hollyhocks & inspected cottages... We lunched there & finished up, Mr. W. calling for us at 4:30.

Fri., Oct 27, 1911
Cold. Clearing. 8:30 started for G.R. having pd. Mrs. Wheeler $16.00 for board, etc & Mr. W. a purse of $2.00. Met brakeman Anderson's family going to a funeral. Nice ride, home at 5 p.m. E.L.C. & Mrs. Whithey welcomed me.

Hollyhocks

1912

Only one Omena entry for the summer months.

Fri., Aug. 9,1912
Returned from Omena, accompanied by Mrs. Pierson. Started in a heavy rain, & left Kate G. at "The Clovers" where her mother will join her.

1913

Mon., June 23, 1913
Pleasant. At 7:30 a.m. Kate Earle & I started [from Grand Rapids] for Omena, arriving at Traverse C. at 2: went to Bank & then took train at 3 & arrived at Mr. Wheeler's at 5:20. Nice, cool, easy trip. ...

Tues., June 24, 1913
Cool morn. Warming up to hot by noon. Had lovely night, good breakfast, ride over to the cottage where Ed. [Deview] met us & we swept & aired & found everything safe & undisturbed by mice or squirrels or tramps. Called at Mrs. Santo's. Siesta this afternoon, & evening on the piazza of Page Cottage.

Page home

Wed., June 25, 1913
Rain. Mr. Wheeler drove us to cottage at 8 o'cl & soon it began to rain, confining us to the house where we mended and sorted linens, etc. Ed. has prepared bed again for transplanting roses. Game of Rhum [rummy]. Letters from fr. Mrs. Grierson, Nelly Miller K, Mary Hinsdill; and yesterday fr. Mary Kendall & F.S.C. [Frederick Stuart Church, the well-known artist, was a cousin of Rebecca]

Thurs., June 26, 1913
Miss Brown rode out & spent the morning with us. Showery. Walked down to pavilion to meet Mr. Wheeler. Restful afternoon. Wrote Mary Richmond & Emma L.C. [Chamberlain] & postmaster Palmer [Walter Miller Palmer of Grand Rapids]. Rhum tonight: she beats me, 19 to 96!!

Fri., June 27, 1913
Hot. Sultry day, partly overcast. Opened Camp Lookout: in pretty good shape. Called on Mrs. Cutcheon ... & on Mrs. Spear & Miss Ring. Mrs. Cloud [Julia] arrived this noon. ...

Sat., June 28, 1913
Hot! Great suffering in cities from hot humidity: 105 degrees in Cinn. Indian took us to The Point this morn. & we rode home in Dittman's auto fast. ... K. [Kate] & I called on the Greene Bros. this eve. & talked village improvement. ...

Omena village scene

Sun., June 29, 1913
Hot. Rain from 4 to 6:30. Hot. Continuous electric storm with copious rain. Sultry during the day & very still. Mr. & Mrs. Weir left for Det. Wrote Mrs. Grierson & Helen Wilkinson. ...

Mon., June 30, 1913
Hot. Rain. Large dining rm opened under the Petersons. ... Ed D. helped at cottages this morn. & Mr. W. advised about repairs. Big wind and rain storm this afternoon. Snow at Duluth.

Tues., July 1, 1913
Mercury dropped about 30 degrees in the night, - cool breezes this morn. Stayed at home this morn. & packed & wrote. The afternoon at the cottages finishing up, and left keys and check for Ed D [Deview] at Anderson's. Heavy wind overtook us as we walked home, but no rain. ...

Wed., July 2, 1913
Very comfortable morn. Much merriment at table about a "Clean Up" Club trying to get Anderson & Greenes to make village neat before the arrival of Gov. [Woodbridge N. Ferris] July 10. ... Took train at 2p.m., arrived G.R. 8:30. E.L.C. [Emma Chamberlain] received me. Hot here! 11 pieces of mail awaiting me.

Sat., July 26, 1913
Warm then hot. ... Wrote to Ed Deview to put Camp Lookout in order for me on Fri. next.

Thurs., July 31, 1913
Torrid. Hot, close night. Gathered all my nerve-power & packed for flight to Omena. A welcome rain came suddenly & followed me to Traverse C. making fine trip & pleasant arrival at Holden's Hotel [William O. Holden was the manager of the Park Place Hotel]. ...

Sat., Aug. 2, 1913
Very busy all day getting two houses settled. Mrs. Townsend & Miss McConnell much pleased.

Sun., Aug. 3, 1913
Such a delightfully quiet day! Reading and writing. Shower prevented our going to Song-Service. ...

Tues., Aug. 5, 1913
Very cool forenoon, just right for weeding my gravel walks, etc. Carpenter here an hr. this afternoon estimating the work I have on hand. Carpenter came at 4:00 p.m. & stayed 'till 5 making estimates, etc.

Wed., Aug. 6, 1913
Fine. Frances Waddell's 11th birthday. Fine. Carpenter Patrick began at 9 a.m. & did fine job at front piazza. I sewing instead of hoeing today. Rev. & Mrs. Hartley called this morn., all nicely settled at Ingall's Bay. ... Frances had bonfire & marshmallow roast on beach tonight. I gave her Hiawatha picture.

Thurs., Aug. 7, 1913
Carpenter at work all day painting & making frame for awning on porch. Quite cool this morn., 60 degrees in house: this afternoon, 75 degrees. The Cong. Ch. had its annual Chicken-pie dinner & social afternoon & evening. Too busy to go, but sent $1.00.

CONGREGATIONAL CHURCH, OMENA RESORT, MICH.

Sat., Aug. 9, 1913
Painter here awhile this morn. Rain this afternoon. Miss Emilie Townsend arrived fr Kal. [Kalamazoo] this morn. We now occupy 4 bedrooms at Camp Lookout.

Sun., Aug. 10, 1913
Pleasant. Fine new moon tonight. Our ladies all went to Pavilion & heard Rev. Devine tell of his Palestine trip.

Mon., Aug. 11, 1913
Squally. Mr. Russell took a launch load to Old Mission Point, to the Kent farm, & they had a rough passage back.

Wed., Aug. 13, 1913
Hazy & bright by turns: sparkling wavelets this noon. Paint on piazza drying nicely. Swept & cleaned some. Rev. & Mrs. Sargent called this afternoon coming in launch fr. opp. shore. Went to "tea" at Sunnyside given by Mrs. Crabtree in honor of her sister, Mrs. Dixon of St. Louis. ...

Fri., Aug. 15, 1913
Spent the evening with Nell Bevier reading letters fr. Eliz. Custer [cousin Libbie], etc.

Sat., Aug. 16, 1913
Finally the paint is sufficiently hard for opening the piazza & I have rugs & cushions out this morn.

Sun., Aug. 17, 1913
Great humidity and absolutely still. In G.R., Chi. , etc., it is much worse, 100 degrees at times. Short of water & many deaths. We have been very quiet all day. No services at the Pavilion on a/c of Indian Camp Meeting, which ends today.

Indian Camp Meeting Grounds, Northport

Launch on Carp Lake (Lake Leelanau)

Mon., Aug. 18, 1913
Some cooler. Intense heat reported still in G.R., Chi., etc. Lecture at Pavilion on foreign travel by Rev. Devine of Det. Gave my tickets to Mrs. Cornell. A lot of our people went to Carp Lake [now Lake Leelanau] fishing. I conducted this morn. a party to "Heart's Ease," Misses Townsend, McConnell & Parsons, all of Kal. Normal, and Mrs. King, and Miss Foster of Ohio.

Tues., Aug. 19, 1913
Such refreshing coolness! This afternoon called at the Russell's & Spears & Ferguson's: the last one occupying "The Garrison." Miss Foster left this morn.

Wed., Aug. 20, 1913
Intense heat reported in cities. Pleasant: nice breeze. Mrs. Townsend went to Traverse by morn. train for a 2 day visit. Elec. light men called, - Abbott & Balch fr. Northport & Leland. ... Our young ladies & their friend, Miss Parsons, picnicked on a rocky beach reached by boat & called for me at 8 o'cl.

Thurs., Aug. 21, 1913
Much cooler. The heat relieved by a stiff breeze all day at The Point, but Mrs. Townsend who came from Trav. C. this eve. reported it very hot there. I invited her & Misses McConnel & Townsend to take tea with me at The Oaks. I worked all day with Ed. D. repairing roof, cutting window, making steps, planting ferns, etc., etc. Lunched at Camp L.

Trillium

Fri., Aug. 22, 1913
Fine rain in night making it lovely & breezy & cool. Planted trilliums early this morn. Wool gown most comfortable. ...

Sun., Aug. 24, 1913
Nice p/c fr. Mary K. [Kendall], weather fine. ... Meals at Camp Lookout on a/c of sore throat etc. Nice fire at Bon. B. [Bonnie Banks] where I have written & read & rec'd call fr. Mrs. Townsend who leaves tomorrow.

Mon., Aug. 25, 1913
High south wind: high sea. Mrs. Townsend returned to G.R. this afternoon. I went to dinner today, 1st meal at Oaks since Sat. noon: break. & tea with the girls.

Tues., Aug. 26, 1913
Cool & nice. Mrs. Jaquez called this morn. & I went with her to call on Prof. & Mrs. Currier at Max Cutcheon's. Girls came on picnic & I lunched on fruit. We all took tea at The Oaks.

Wed., Aug. 27, 1913
Cool. Pleasant. Prof. & Mrs. Currier called this morn. & enjoyed my wood fire. Nice long letter fr. Mary describing entertainments & enclosed one fr. Russll's wife: all prospering, glad. Girls went to Clovers this p.m. I am very busy packing.

Thurs., Aug. 28, 1913
Threatening, wind & clouds from South. Such a hustling time with Deview & Emilie T. [Townsend] to help close Bonnie B. Lunched at Camp Lookout & off at 1:20 with the Russells for Trav. City. They went on & I stop overnight. ...

Fri., Aug. 29, 1913 - Traverse City for dinner; G.R. at 9 p.m.
Cool & variable. Spent pleasant morn. writing, then at Bank, making depos. etc., then shopping, and dinner: shower this afternoon. Off for Walton at 2:40, Peck [Alphonso] & Anderson's [John H.] train. Smooth ride to G.R. when Emma L.C. welcomed me at 9 p.m.

1914

Wed., May 6, 1914
... Letter from Miss Wier fr. Omena where they located in Camp Lookout & found it most satisfactory, fires lighted by Deview etc. Sent first month's rent. ...

Thurs., May 14, 1914
... Wrote Mrs. Wiley about rooms at "The Towers."

Sat., May 16, 1914
... Letter fr. Mr. Wheeler about Omena pump wh. I ans'd at once. ...

Wed., May 20, 1914
... Mrs. Baker [Ellen L.] ... to go to Omena without me on Friday.

Fri., May 22, 1914
... Mrs. Baker was to go to Mr. Wheeler's till I arrive.

Wed., May 27, 1914 - En route to Omena
Thunder-showers in night made delightful change. Started in rain [from G.R.] at 7:15, had delightful trip & arrived at Omena at 5:30. At Traverse City mailed p/c to E.L.C. [Emma Chamberlain], dep. $20.84 in Bank, shopped a little, met with Mr. & Mrs. Wheeler & was welcomed at station by Mrs. Baker. ...

Thurs., May 28, 1914
Pleasant. Mrs. Baker & I walked over to the Point & opened up Bonnie Banks finding all OK. Regulated some this morn. Lunched under Cedar trees & then slept in hammock etc. Mr. Wheeler came & inspected pump & found all right. Dreadful disaster in the St. Lawrence River! Collision & 1200 lives lost fr. "Empress of Ireland."

Fri., May 29, 1914
Rain last night & this afternoon. Walked out to cottage this morn. and worked 2 hours with Ben Bursell: then Mrs. Baker came & trimmed my new arch with bean vines, then we lunched with Mrs. Weir: then decorated parlor. Mr. Wheeler met us half way home. Letter from Cous. Eliz. Custer from Peking, China. Mailed letter to sister M. [Mary] this morn.

Sat., May 30, 1914
Pretty breezy: Benny and I spent an hour burning worms' nests on the beach this morning. The orchards have been infected by them, farmers fighting vigorously & many at edges of the wood. Soldiers' Memorial Day Celebration at Northport.

Sun., May 31, 1914
Quiet day at home: grey, threatening rain. After church this afternoon Mrs. Wiley called and drove Mrs. B. [Baker] and me to "The Towers" where we took tea and inspected the place, arranging to come to her Tues. eve. ... Walked home in the moonlight.

Mon., June 1, 1914
Deview had the contract for moving my pump, advised by Mr. Wheeler. Settled with Ed. Deview to date for pumpwork, care of cottage, etc. Letter fr. Eliz. Custer fr. China.

Tues., June 2, 1914
Cool breezy. Mrs. B. [Baker] went into Wheeler's woods with Benny & dug flowers to send to G. Rapids. I walked to the Point & met Walter Barth & planned for painting. Lunched with the Weirs and spent afternoon assisting Julien Deview in mopping the house floors fr. top to bottom & spreading rugs. Mr. Wheeler called for me at 4:30. After super we packed our grips, bade good-by to Sunset Lodge & rode with Mrs. Wiley to The Towers, on Boulder Terrace where we hope to be for a week.

Wed., June 3, 1914
Rain after noon. Mrs. Baker & I explored Dr. Weaver's grounds this morn: trout brook, woodland, sandy beach, orchard, serpentine drive, white birch grove, terrace of wildflowers, handsome 2 story bungalow. Afternoon by open fire in the large living room. ...

General Benjamin H. Grierson's cottage, the Garrison

Thurs., June 4, 1914
Damp & grey. At The Towers all day. Wrote Cous. Mary R. [Richmond] ack. genealogical books. Mrs. Wiley & Mrs. Baker rode over to the Point & brought Mrs. Weir & daughter to dine here & then go to Club - meeting at Mrs. Patrick's.

Fri., June 5, 1914
Pleasant: cool & bright. Mrs. B. and I rode over to The Point & transplanted wildflowers this morn. Walter Barth worked for me for 3 hrs. this afternoon fixing stairs & graveling paths. Lunch with Weirs.

Sat., June 6, 1914
Just like an April day: bright sunrise: after 8 a.m. changeable: at 6 p.m. sharp thunder storm. Mrs. Wiley took us to Bonnie B. this morn. & came for us at 4 p.m. I cleaned lamps & put things generally in order.

Sun., June 7, 1914
Hot. Spent morn. as quietly as possible. This afternoon Mr. Wiley took the family in his surrey over to The Point and we made the sad entrance to "The Garrison" whose cordial entertainers (Gen'l Grierson & wife & Mrs. Cavender) are gone forever.

Mon., June 8, 1914
Very comfortable. Went alone to cottage & met Walter Barth who painted piazza & sills: lunched with Mrs. Weir.

Tues., June 10, 1914 - Omena leaving: G.R. today
Cool morning, very nice for our exit from "The Towers." Bade Mr. & Mrs. Wiley adieu & Miss Sparling drove us to the train ... Pretty hot on train but good breeze. ... Found things in status quo at Elmwood, no repairs done in my room.

Tues., June 23, 1914
[Rebecca left for trip to Detroit, Canada, Buffalo, Rochester, Auburn; back to Grand Rapids by July 2]
Hot! Very hot & humid. Hard work getting off for Auburn. ... Mr. Bird took me to train at 5, and at 10, I am in Detroit ready to tunnel it to Canada en route to Auburn to see Aunt Nancy [Eagles].

Wed., July 8, 1914
Cooler. Packing today. Selected carpet for bed-room. Otis B. bought ticket for Omena & took charge of my safe-box key, to which I have a duplicate no. 161. Wrote to Park Hotel, Mrs. Pierson, Postmaster Omena Kalchik. Gave Mrs. Hall, my opp. neighbor, one of F.S.C.'s [Frederick Stuart Church] photogravures. Called at Earles this eve.

Thurs., July 9, 1914 - Traverse
Pleasant, cool morn. for finishing packing etc. Pd. Mrs. Noble to date & rewarded Kathleen for helping me off: pretty feeble after late journey & illness. Pretty hot at noon; train at 1:30 bringing me comfortably to Trav. City at 7:30. Mr. & Mrs. Holden & Mildred in dining rm. greeted me.

Fri., July 10, 1914
Fine night's rest. Went to Co. store [Hannah & Lay Mercantile] after breakfast & ordered awning etc. and boarded train at 10:20 with new conductor Stuart [S.W.] ... Arr. at Omena at 11:30 & rode to Bonnie Banks in an automobile: then to Oaks to dinner, meeting Bevier, Crabtree & family, Mrs. Cutcheon & Wheelers.

Sat., July 11, 1914
Pleasant. Mrs. Pierson arrived this noon to visit at "Bonnie Banks" 10 days. Also came to Camp Lookout, a Mrs. Capes fr. Chicago. Mr. & Mrs. Chas. Blair & 3 children came to "The Oaks." ...

Sun., July 12, 1914
Feel pretty slow after the all-night storm fr. 10 p.m. till 6 a.m., with almost continuous lightning. It cleared this morn. at about 10. Good naps this afternoon & after that readings on my piazza, - Mr. Gray's letters fr. the Orient, etc. I breakfasted next door, dinner at Oaks. No tea.

Mon., July 13, 1914
Cool morn. & eve. Hot at noon. Arranged new awning this morn myself, no boy appearing to help me. Breakfast at Camp Lookout, dinner at Oaks, tea at Mrs. Cutcheon's where Mrs. Pierson & I met Mr. Max C. [Cutcheon], Mrs. Dittman, Mrs. Spear, Miss Ring, Miss Fitz, Mrs. Russell, then called on Miss Bevier & the Weirs & Mrs. Capes.

Tues., July 14, 1914
Put up green awning by myself. Very comfortable day. ... Mrs. Jaquez called this forenoon & I took her to "The Oaks" to dinner. I had as guests at my table Mrs. Weir & daughter & their friend, Mrs. Capes of Chicago. Cool eve. making my front porch very acceptable at sunset, and Miss Bevier & Mrs. Brown shared it with us.

Wed., July 15, 1914
The National Pike Commission [West Michigan Pike Association] with Gov. Ferris, occupying a doz. automobiles passed thru today, rounding the Point. Wrote Sister Mary & Emma Earle. Mr. & Mrs. Chas. Blair spent the eve, on my piazza.

Pike Tourists are Welcome at
OMENA — THE RESORT IDEAL

Boating Bathing Fishing
Five justly popular Resort Hotels

"The Most Beautiful View on the Pike"
is that from
"*The LEELANAU*"
Its Dinners are Famous.
Mine Host Campbell Knows How.

For information, cottages, etc., address
JOHN R. SANTO or THE POSTMASTER
Gasoline and Lubricants Obtainable Here

Note the West Michigan Pike sign on the telephone pole.
Gov. Woodbridge Ferris stopped and spoke
in Omena in 1914

Thurs., July 16, 1914
Just a week this morn since I came. Hot & still until 2 p.m. when a lovley breeze refreshed us. Wrote Lay Co. [Hannah & Lay Mercantile] sending check for awning & thermos $4.40. Wrote Aunt N.R.E. [Nancy Eagles] sending $35.00 to pay for expansion to her piazza. Wrote Mrs. Baker describing conditions here. Mrs. Pierson has good news from home, and she begins this eve. some inprovements at her cottage here.

Fri., July 17, 1914
Cold. Mercury dropped from 80 to 50 degrees. High wind this forenoon. This afternoon went with Mrs. Pierson & Mrs. Brown to the orchard for Black-eyed Susans. This eve. hearth fire, and to the neighbors who came in ... Mrs. Pierson read extracts from her own Nature Books.

Clara D. Pierson

Sun., July 19, 1914
Lovely "Omena Weather": very quiet day. Wrote Sister Mary & sent it to Traverse City by Miss Clark.. Mr. Sargent sends me "Eve. Press" article on "The New Pantlind."...

Tues., July 21, 1914
Invited several to a reading this afternoon, but it became so hot at noon that we recalled the invitations. Max Cutcheon & wife spent the eve. on our piazza: I hung out our Chinese Lanterns.

Wed., July 22, 1914
Hot & windy. Rec'd receipt for my memorial gift to the State Y.M.C.A., $3,000, an endowment in honor of my father, a prominent pioneer of 1836. ...

Thurs., July 23, 1914
Fine quiet rain last night: not so hot today. Mrs. Pierson dined at "The Leelanau" with Mrs. Mack. I visited with Miss Bevier after dinner then came home & sewed & wrote a letter to Clara Sanford enclosing check for $50 for her & her sister Gertrude to use in going fr. Ithaca to Auburn to care for Aunt Nancy. Met at tea-table Mrs. Cutcheon & Wheeler & Pierson: we called on Hibbards [Hibberds], then Bradleys called on us & invited us to tea tomorrow: regretted.

Fri., July 24, 1914
Comfortable weather. Mrs. Pierson departs. We dined together for the last time at noon. Then Mrs. Pierson rode with Mr. Hibbard [Hibberd] to the train, en route for G.R. where she will spend the night at "The Mertons," then to Stanton tomorrow. I visited with Miss Bevier after dinner, then nap in hammock. ...

Sat., July 25, 1914
Slept last night at Camp L. after supping with the Weirs. Did repairing today on pillows, sheets, etc., etc. Pd. Mrs. Pierson's & my bills at the "The Oaks" for 2 weeks, $19 including all of Thursday & Fri. dinners. My next bill begins today.

Sun., July 26, 1914
Turned quite cool in night - warm again today, but a fine breeze fr. the Bay.

Tues., July 28, 1914
Cool & nice. Called this afternoon on all the people on Morningside Terrace, - Powers, Spears, Russells, Cutcheons, Crabtrees, Waddells: took tea at The Oaks & then called at The Graves. ...

Graves cottage

Wed., July 29, 1914
Cool, Omena day, bright & nice breeze. Quiet day with me. Mrs. Blair & Margaret, the young art student, left for home this noon. I lent the latter one of my art magazines. Found Mrs. Cutcheon "The Way of an Indian."...

Fri., July 31, 1914
Busy all day superintending work on the roof of Camp L. Mr. Krohn is replacing shingles, adding eaves-troughs and ridge boards, the last being of metal. ... Sleep the last tonight at Camp L.; Gertrude, our waitress will sleep with me now at Bonnie B. until next guest comes. The Weirs and I are preparing for their next guests.

Sat., Aug. 1, 1914
Will I live to write today? If alive, will I be able to write? Yes, I am gratefully here yet, in much better health than I dared to hope. Mr. Krohn finished the roof of Camp L. & I paid him $5.90 for the 2 days work. Mrs. Anderson and George's bride took tea with me at Oaks & visited the Cutcheons piazza later.

Cutcheon cottage

Sun., Aug. 2, 1914
1870 - My father went to our mysterious home today [referring to her father's death]: so many of the good old friends are over there. Fine, clear, cool day after a heavy rain in the night. Fire on hearth this morn. Mr. & Mrs. Pratt arrived at Camp L. fr. Chicago. I dined and supped at "The Oaks," Rev. & Mrs. Sargent walked over fr. The Clovers this morning.

Mon., Aug. 3, 1914
Cool: so thankful. Breakfast this morn. with the Weirs & Pratts, and tea there by invitation. At dinner introduced Mr. Pratt to several friends. Very busy morning putting the house in good order for next guest. Gertrude, our waitress has slept three nights at my house; pd. her 75 cents.

Tues., Aug. 4, 1914
Cool morn: fire on hearth. Breakfast next door: other meals at Oaks: Miss Pollard arrived in time for dinner: after tea at Oaks we and Mr. Pratt walked home with Mrs. Cutcheon & Mrs. Wheeler & saw the full moon rise. ...

Thurs., Aug. 6, 1914
High winds but soft air. Omena Day at village. Pres. Wilson's wife very ill with chronic disease! Died at 5 p.m. at the White House, Washington.

Fri., Aug. 7, 1914
Perfect Omena day. Pd. Mrs. Weir in full for a/c breakfasts, $1.00. Rec'd fr. her rent for Aug. $20.84 ... Miss Pollard went to "The Clovers" for a row-boat. After dinner Mr. & Mrs. Pratt walked thru the woods with us. ...

Sat., Aug. 8, 1914
Wrote Mrs. Pierson thanking her for seeds, etc. ... I am not at all well today.

Sun., Aug 9, 1914
Hot & sultry. No better: did not go to meals. Miss Pollard went to Cong Ch. with several others this afternoon. Rev. Geo. Sargent led the service admirably & gave a little talk for a hot day.

Wed., Aug 12, 1914
Miss P. [Pollard] brought me dinner on a tray: I went to tea at Oaks. Break. at Weirs. ...

Thurs., Aug. 13, 1914
Specially cold. Mr. Pratt and I spent part of forenoon trimming trees on upper terrace & putting sky parlor in shape for services on Sunday morn. Rev. Sargent's sprained ankle later prevented service, alas! Great threat of rain: nil.

Fri., Aug. 14, 1914
Cool & partly cloudy: rain this eve. We were so sorry to part with our friends, Mr. & Mrs. Ashton Pratt who left this noon for Colorado. Mrs. Sargent & Miss Torrence called to tell of Rev. S. sprained ankle. Miss Pollard went to Indian Camp meeting with Mrs. Cutcheon. Rain this eve.

Sat., Aug. 15, 1914
Cool & breezy. Benny worked for me this morn. We had great time with squirrels dislodging 2 from my upper ceiling, me a flying squirrel. 2 meals at Oaks.

Mon., Aug. 17, 1914
Pd. Mrs. Kalchik of "The Oaks" to date; also Mrs. Weir $2.00 for meals. Pretty busy arranging cottage to leave etc. Took tea at Oaks, then Mr. Kalchik drove us over to Wheeler's for the night & Miss Spicer gave us nice rooms in cottage, Miss Pollard & I.

Tues., Aug. 18, 1914
Heavy rains & electrical storms all night, but we were happy because so well sheltered. After good breakfast, Mr. Wheeler drove us to station at 8 o'cl. Comfortable run to G. Rapids, cool & wet till half way down: hot on arrival at 5:30. Geo. Bird met us with auto - found rooms ready. ...

Grand Rapids & Indiana train made frequent runs
between Grand Rapids & Mackinaw City

Fri., Sept. 11, 1914
Cold & grey. Wrote Mr. Wheeler & Mrs. Weir and Mrs. Deview to expect me at Omena on the 15th. Wrote John Moran to be ready with report on my return, about 22nd. Mrs. Pierson of Stanton called this afternoon. ...

Mon., Sept. 14, 1914 - G.R. to Traverse City
Pleasant. Had dreary, uncomfortable night, but in the fresh morning air took the quickstep & got ready for my trip by noon. Pd. Mrs. Noble [Rebecca's landlady] $31.00 for the past month's board & several guests. Took train at 1:30; nice run to Walton where brakeman Anderson [John H.] greeted me, then to Traverse & Park Hotel where Mr. Holden & Miss [Nell] Bevier gave me welcome.

Tues., Sept. 15, 1914
Beautiful day, cool & fresh after heavy rain. Nice breakfast, good visit with Miss Bevier, train at 10:30 for Omena under conductor Stuart [S.W.]. Marie met me at station. ... Called this afternoon at Deview's to arrange for work; also at Porter's & Geo. Anderson's.

Grand Rapids & Indiana depot at Traverse City

Wed., Sept. 16, 1914
Beautiful day! Rode out to Bonnie Banks with Mr. Hibbard [Hibberd] & Miss Weir. Opened cottages & made a beginning towards regulating for closing. One good hammock nap. Walked home, part way with Mrs. Porter. The Browns gone to Cinn., the Whitneys to Chi., - Porters & I alone here.

Thurs., Sept. 17, 1914
Partly cloudy & sultry. Put in a fine day's work with Deview, mending the roofs of both cottages, cleaning & bringing in porch furniture, taking down awnings, etc. Rode out with Geo. Anderson & Mr. Hibbard [Hibberd] brot [brought] me home at evening. Lunched at Weirs with Mrs. Max Cutcheon. Letters fr. Aunt Nancy, cousins Mary R. & Mary Church and Emma L.C. [Chamberlain]

Fri., Sept. 18, 1914
Overcast most of the day: hot when sun shone. Rode over with Geo. Anderson, having made purchases. ... Deview spent day repairing stairs leading fr. beach, fixing locks & window shades, etc., etc. Lunch with Weirs.

Sat., Sept. 19, 1914
Beautiful morn.: with the breeze in my face I walked to Bonnie B. & in the same pleasant fashion came back this eve. as far as the Porters where I embarked in their fine canoe & rode with them to the village dock. Did a good day's work, lunching with Mrs. Weir and consulting about the closing of Camp L. She will remain one week longer.

Glimpse of the Point

Sun., Sept. 20, 1914
Hot. Very quiet morn writing letters ... Mrs. Wiley quite ill, so the Clouds & Hibbards [Hibberds] & Barters & Miss Russell & the Weirs took dinner with us at Peterson's Cafe: also a dozen peach packers. ...

Mon., Sept. 21, 1914
Hot. Restless night: heat & nervousness. Breakfasted & said good-bye to Prof. & Mrs. Porter & Harold & dog Jerry. Mr. Hibbard [Hibberd] took me to The Point in his car, arriving at 8:15. Fine breeze arose at about 9 & remained thru day. I worked hard & got all well done at 5; rode back with Hibbards [Hibberds] & tea with Mrs. Peterson, manager. The 10-acre peach orchard of Mr. W. [Wheeler] ripened so suddenly that he & a big force of men & women had to work all day Sunday.

Tues., Sept. 22, 1914
Cool. Rain in the night & showers this morn. Last breakfast at Sunset Lodge & Marie escorted me to station ... Mr. Barth rode with me to Traverse & here I met Miss Bevier for an hour's visit. She stays at Park Hotel for the present. Bid adieu to Conductor Stuart & brakeman Anderson & on main road met friends of Mrs. Wheeler & Miss Pollard, Mrs. Miller. Arr. at Elmwood [in Grand Rapids] at 5:45.

1915

Fri., June 18, 1915 - start [for] Omena
... Mr. & Mrs. Torrey & I started at 2 p.m. for Omena. Rain hard fr. 4 to 5. At Walton met our good friends, Peck & Anderson. Arr. Park Pl. Hotel & welcomed by Mr. Holden at 8:20.

Sat., June 19, 1915
Bright, bracing day. Ran down to bank & after breakfast & [with] the Torreys inspected main street. At 10:30 off, & arrived at Omena at noon & whisked over to The Point in Auto. Dined at the Oaks with Piersons, Bevier & Crabtrees.

Sun., June 20, 1915
Pleasant. At Bonnie Banks for a quiet Sunday. Glad to see our old friends on Morningside Terrace & the Hibbards [Hibberds] at The Wigwam. ...

Mon., June 21, 1915
Bright & early at Bonnie Banks & got piazzas & sitting rooms in order. Very cold: fireplace & hot water bottle in constant use. Rain this eve. Cards this eve.

Tues., June 22, 1915
Greeting fr. Aunt Nancy. [Eagles] Partly sunny, but cold. Inspected Mr. & Mrs. Santos's cottages this afternoon & walked across the rustic bridge & into the Indian Garden then thru Woodland Way home. Showers this eve.

Wed., June 23, 1915
Cold. Quite like old Omena, bright. This afternoon drove over to "The Clovers" & The Leelanau & saw the Sargent cottage: Mr. & Mrs. Torrey & Miss Bevier. Walked along front st. this morn. & called on Mrs. Pierson & Mrs. Dillingham.

Thurs., June 24, 1915
Showery & cold. Birth-card from Mary K. [Kendall]. Evergreen trimming & picture show in house. Invitation fr. Towers. Nice quiet & story-telling match in parlor of Oaks after dinner with Pierson, Dillingham & Torreys. Letter fr. Libbie C. [Custer]

Sun., June 27, 1915
Spent pleasant morn, in writing at cottage - Sister Mary.

Tues., June 29, 1915
Warm & fine. Box of cherries fr. Mr. Torrey this noon which I shared with others. ... Called on Mrs. Ed. Deane in Cutcheon cottage this eve.

Wed., June 30, 1915
... Deview helped me all day & I pd. his bill for care during the winter & the present, $14.50. We cleared "Woodland Way," gathered gravel, arranged Camp Lookout, fixed arches & fences, put up awnings etc.

Fri., July 2, 1915
Warm, sunny morning, showery afternoon & much cooler: fire in hearth this eve, & Miss Bevier & I played Ruhm [Rummy]. Wrote Mrs. Cutcheon at the cottage. Mrs. Hibbard [Hibberd] & guest called.

Sat., July 3, 1915
Cold & sunny. Spent forenoon repairing Old Glory & making rustic fence. Letter fr. Mary K. Mr. Ed Deane arrived fr. G.R. to spent 4th with his family in Cutcheon cottage. Called on him after tea & saw fireworks of children on Grierson dock.

Sun., July 4, 1915
Nor'east storm. Queer Fourth! Began raining at 9 a.m. I spent morn. at cottage: call fr. Mr. & Mrs. Ruth, had Mr. & Mrs. Ed. Deane to dine after which we had a meeting with Piersons, Crabtrees, Ruths, & Bevier in the sitting rm and sang Kate Hale's "Columbia" & heard the story of the Cutcheon-Currier flag-raising & Mrs. Currier's poem. ...

Mon., July 5, 1915
Mr. & Mrs. Hamilton arrived last eve, guests of the Deane's: room & dined at the Oaks, called on me & left after tea at Deane's. Busy in cottage with fire for it is real cold.

Tues., July 6, 1915
Sunny but cool. Began clearing The Trail this morn. & transplanted some flowers. ... Mr & Mrs. Seydel in their car brought to call on us - Mrs. Gay Perkins & Mrs. Ward.

Wed., July 7, 1915
Heavy rain last night, damp & grey today. Sewing & writing at Bonnie Banks. Sent cards to Dr. Hooker, P.O. carrier Singer and Mrs. Noble. Just as cold in G.R. as here.

Thurs., July 8, 1915
Clear & warm. Went to village this morning & called at Wheelers & pd. bills to date at Anderson's. All afternoon regulating Camp Lookout's windows, shades, curtains, etc. Very destructive cyclone in Cincinnati, 21 killed.

Fri., July 9, 1915
Fine. Decided not to go home tomorrow but wait until Tuesday & finish Camp Lookout. Ride in jitney to my cottage. Teleph. by Frank Anderson to Geo. Bird who will tel. to Mrs. Noble.

Dittman cottage

Sat., July 10, 1915
Sultry. Spent day at cottages, eve. at Miss Bevier's. Circus at Trav. City. Rain tonight.

Sun., July 11, 1915
Perfectly quiet & hazy. Wrote to Mary Kendall, Mrs. Noble, Miss Yerkes, Mrs. Lowe. Mrs. Spear & Miss Ring dined with me. The Bents & Parsons have come to the Log Cabin. Called at Dittman's & Pierson's.

Mon., July 12, 1915
Fine. Fog on bay last night. Very busy morn. with Deview & Indian: fence, woodshed, cedar dec., curtains, blazed trail, etc. Matinee under Saxton cedars at 2 p.m. by the children. P/c to F.S.C. [Frederick Stuart Church]

Tues., July 13, 1915
Hot. Finished work at cottages & dressed for tea. Mrs. Spear & Miss Ring called this eve. on upper piazza. ...

Wed., July 14, 1915 - to Grand R. fr. Omena
Hot morn. Pd. bill at the Oaks, $18.04 after breakfast with Miss Bevier & Henry took me to 8:50 train under Stuart [S.W.] & arr. at Trav. C. at 10:30, took train under Peck [Alphonso] & Anderson [John H.] for G.R. Cloudy sky & nice breeze. Arr. G.R. at 4:50. Dinner at Elmwood.

Sat., July 17, 1915
... Letter fr. Nell Bevier: no guests at "Oaks" yet.

Mon., July 19, 1915
... Took to Helen Hunt a card for help on her trip to Omena tomorrow & note to Pierson.

Sat., July 24, 1915
Chicago excursionists die. ... "Eastland" with 2000 on board sunk in Chi. River & half of them drowned this morn.

Thurs., July 29, 1915
Very warm. Mrs. Johnston has motored to Traverse & Omena with the Slighs. ... Wire fr. Omena asking me to ad [advertise] "The Oaks."

Fri., July 30, 1915
... Advertised "The Oaks" for Mr. Kalchik. ...

Sat., Aug. 7, 1915
Warmer & sultry. Wrote to Park Hotel, Traverse, for 2 rooms for Mon night.

Mon., Aug. 9, 1915
Pleasant. Started for Omena at 2:10 accompanied by Miss Ellen Morrison as my guest. Very agreeable trip to Cadillac: while at supper her sister, Mrs. Webber & son greeted us. Arr. at Park Hotel at 8:30.

Tues., Aug. 10, 1915
Pleasant. Went to the Bank & Co. store after breakfast, then to train at 10:30 and off for Omena with Con. [conductor] Stuart. Arr. at 12 & drove to Oaks to dinner: heartily welcomed. No key to Bonnie B. so we are settled at Camp Lookout.

Wed., Aug. 11, 1915
Pleasant. Deview sent keys this afternoon so we opened & aired cottage. Called this eve. on Dr. Heston at Pierson's: she has seen the cousins recently in Cal. & goes on tomorrow. Fine game of Rhum this eve.

Thurs., Aug. 12, 1915
Fine weather for Omena Day with chicken-pie dinner in the village & games, to which most of our people went. Miss M. [Morrison] & I moved over to Bonnie Banks this morn. & Deview fixed the roof. P/c fr. Mary K. [Kendall] fr. Santa Barbara en route for home. Mrs. Pierson ill.

Fri., Aug. 13, 1915
New moon. Mild and mostly sunny. We both had a fine night: pleasant walk to breakfast. ... Fine piazza days, we played Halma dice. Nice Mrs. Powers of Evanston called this afternoon ...

Sun., Aug. 15, 1915
Warm, but breezy. At home all day. ...

Tues., Aug. 17, 1915
Clear cold. Fine day for out-door work. Ed. Deview spent day pulling poison ivy, cutting weeds, clearing wood, shed etc. Pd. him in full to date by Traverse check $8.15. Letter fr. Libbie Custer, San Fran. Hurricane at Galveston great damage & death.

Wed., Aug. 18, 1915
Fine. Outdoor work this morn. ... Walked to Leelanau Hotel this afternoon & met Rev. & Mrs. Sargent who walked to Oaks with us. Halma this eve.

Thurs., Aug. 19, 1915
Pleasant. Transplanting this morn. ... Walked to Heart's Ease this afternoon & thru the Palmer Path to Pierson's calling on her & her mother. Reading & Rhum this eve.

Fri., Aug. 20, 1915
Fine. Miscellaneous morning. This afternoon Mr. Kalchik took Miss M., Nell B. [Bevier] & me to drive on the opposite side of the Bay, calling on the Sargents & Keene's [spelling?] at "The Clovers," then up & down hill. Wrote 2 notes to Traverse about lantern.

Sun., Aug. 22, 1915
Fine! Mrs. Wilkinson arriv. before dinner fr. Manistee. Room for her at the Hotel. Calls fr. Mrs. Towers & Miss Newton & Mr. & Mrs. Ruth. ... Called on Mrs. Spear & friends.

Mon., Aug. 23, 1915
Threatening & breezy, Mr. & Mrs. Sargent called this morn. Mrs. Wilkinson came over for an hour. Called on the Hibbards [Hibberds].

Tues., Aug. 24, 1915
... Threatening rain. Miss Morrison got off this morn. at 9, & Mrs. Wilkinson moved over. We attended a lovely gathering of the Colony for tea at Mrs. Spear's & Miss Ring's this afternoon.

Wed., Aug. 25, 1915
Pd. board bill. Grey morn. Sunny afternoon, high winds. Could not accept Rev. Sargent's invitation to drive to the lighthouse. Mrs. W. [Wilkinson] in bed all day with headache. ... Coldest in 25 years.

Fri., Aug. 27, 1915
Frost killed potatoes & corn. 44 to 60 [degrees]. Beautiful, sunny crisp day. Busy packing, preparatory to going to Traverse with Mrs. W. tomorrow. Mrs. Hibbard [Hibberd] called this afternoon. Pd. Anderson to date. Rev. Sargent called this eve.

Sat., Aug. 28, 1915
Pleasant. Mr. Deview helped do the final closing this morn. & I pd. him in full & left keys. Pd. Hotel at dinner $11.00 & took 2 o'cl. train, landing in at Traverse & Park Hotel at 4. Wrote Sister Mary. Met Robt. Bradley going to his wedding at Omena.

Sun., Aug. 29, 1915 - Traverse City
Aren't we glad we are out of the woods! Raining here this afternoon & cold. We went to Grace Ch. & heard one of Bp. McWilliams good sermons ... and very nice music by a vested boy & choir & violin: Then to look at the windows in the new Methodist Ch. Mrs. W. dined at Dr. Munson's. Wrote to Nell Bevier.

Mon., Aug. 30, 1915
Crisp & sunny. We have taken it easy today, strolling & feasting: music this eve. in Mrs. Holden's room. ...

Tues., Aug. 31, 1915
Pleasant: just the right temperature for travel in wool suits. Mrs. W. started for Manistee at 9:30 & I at 10:30 for G.R. ... Had such a comfortable trip, knowing no one & Geo. Bird met me at home station with taxi. All well at Elmwood.

Fould's Log Cabin, Omena, Mich.

1916

Tues., June 13, 1916
Pleasant. Mrs. Baker & I en route for Omena, 2:10 fr. G.R. met Conductor Peck [Alphonso] & brakeman Anderson [John H.] at Walton Junc., the former 30 years in G.R. & I service, retires on pension in Sept. Park Hotel at 8 o'cl. Rain in the night.

Wed., June 14, 1916 - "The Oaks" - Omena
Bright & lovely after 9 a.m. Went to Bank & dep. $100, train at 10:30, Omena at 12. Kalchik met us with new auto. Mr. & Mrs. Lotspeich & 2 children joined us for "The Oaks' meals, & Fould cottage. Miss Bevier, Mrs. Crabtree, Mrs. Waddell & Frances boarding here. Gertrude, the waitress & Primeau clerk.

Thurs., June 15, 1916
Pleasant. Opened cottage yesterday, finding all right. Went this morn. to "Bonnie Banks" & put it in general order. We like the family from Cinn. very much: he an instructor in German in the U. of Ohio.

Fri., June 16, 1916
Heavy rain in the night & again this afternoon: everything soaked. Bah! Hotel rooms enlarged & better equipped & table fine. Sent p/c to Emma C. [Chamberlain]

Sat., June 17, 1916
Rain. Cold & grey & more rain in night. Transplanted flowers & moved all mattresses up stairs to air & dry. Afternoon at hotel by fire. Wrote to Sister Mary & Bp. McC, [McCormick] pledge for Akeley $300. [Akeley Hall was a boarding school for girls in Grand Haven affiliated with the Episcopal Church]

Sun., June 18, 1916
More cold & grey. Morning by hotel fire. The Spears here to dinner at our table, & the Prof. Lotspeich & family came from Leelanau Heights for the last time. This afternoon we called at the Santo's & Crabtree's where Mrs. Waddell & daughter are.

Mon., June 19, 1916
Colder night than ever. Mrs. B. [Baker] and I spent morn. transplanting wildflowers. This afternoon rode with Mrs. Crabtree and Mrs. Waddell to Northport Point.

Tues., June 20, 1916
Sunny. Cold & clear. Mrs. Baker left for G. Rapids at 8:30 this morn. I spent forenoon at inn, and wrote to Mrs. Cutcheon and Elizabeth Thompson. Aftern. at Cottage, preparing for Deview.

Wed., June 21, 1916
Cold & clear. Morn. at inn. Wrote Mrs. Eugene Babcock & Mrs. Cecilia Follett: invited the former to Camp L. for July.

Thurs., June 22, 1916
Strenuous morn. Finishing up with Deview & pd. $42.75. This afternoon drove over & called on Dr. & Mrs. Weaver & Mr. & Mrs. Sargent.

Fri., June 23, 1916 - Omena to G.R.
Thunderstorm in early morn. Rode to station in rain. ... Arrived home at 5 p.m. Good trip...

Fri., Aug. 18, 1916
... The Cotton family delighted with Camp Lookout wh. I have loaned them. ...

Wed., Aug. 23, 1916
... Wrote Mrs. Wilkinson about Omena after 4th approx. Wrote Miss Primeau of "The Oaks."

Mon., Sept. 4, 1916 - Labor Day
Wrote to Mrs. Wilkinson & Sister Mary & mailed en route to train for Traverse City at 2 p.m. Pd. Mrs. Noble to date, $18.35. Nice trip, plenty room, no dust. Met Anderson at Walton, but Peck has been retired on a pension after 35 yrs. service, 70 yrs. old. Arr. at Park Hotel at 8 o'cl.

Tues., Sept. 5, 1916
Nice night, comfortable morn. Wrote Eliz. B. C. [Custer] & E.L.C. [Emma Chamberlain] Train at 11 o'cl, Omena at 12:30, dinner at The Oaks with the Crabtrees & Miss Bevier. Expected to find Mrs. Wilkinson here, but no! Spent afternoon at Bonnie B. & called on Crabtrees.

Nagonaba St., Northport

Wed., Sept. 6, 1916
Lovely June-like day. Spent morn. at Bonnie Banks cleaning out store. closet. Rec'd several letters. ...

Thurs., Sept. 7, 1916
Sent wire to E.L.C. that I would not be in G.R. till Tues p.m.

Fri., Sept. 8, 1916
Sent p/c to E.L.C. Rode to Northport with Mr. & Mrs. Hibbard [Hibberd], then an hour at Bonnie B. & then welcomed Mrs. Wilkinson.

Sat., Sept. 9, 1916
Lovely day. Julien [Deview] came & we completed the closing of Camp Lookout. This afternoon Mrs. W. [Wilkinson] and I sorted pamphlets, music & pictures. The Palmer family went home this eve. One son has bot [bought] the Cutcheon cottage.

Sun., Sept. 10, 1916
Pleasant. Mrs. W. and I at cottage looking over historical papers, photos, etc. Mrs. Crabtree & nieces, Wadsworth & Ayars left on the eve. train for Chi. & Jacksonville. High winds threatening rain.

Mon., Sept. 11, 1916
Pleasant but sultry. Miss Bevier went to Traverse at noon. We packed box for Akeley this morn., hung pictures at Oaks this afternoon, Rhum this eve.

Tues., Sept. 12, 1916
Rain in night. Mr. Kalchik helped close cottages this morn, then went away and Louis Anderson took us to station at 1 o'cl. I left my watch, he to send it by mail. Mrs. W. & I to Traverse, then she to Manistee train & I to G.R. & I. ...

Omena Station

1917

Tues., July 17, 1917
Packing for Omena. Rainy day. Pd. several bills, Richards, Bermans, etc. Gave Mrs. Noble military picture.

Wed., July 18, 1917 - start for Omena
Rain. Mrs. Vercoe & I started at 2:20 for Traverse, rain hard till Cadillac. Met Anderson. Mr. V. [Vercoe] met us at Park Hotel. I have invited them as my guests for 2 weeks at Camp Lookout, they to give me breakfast & tea, & I to give them dinner at The Oaks ...

Thurs., July 19, 1917
Fine night, lovely morn. Sent card to E.L.C. [Emma Chamberlain]: met Miss Elliott & we walked down to Co. Store [Hannah & Lay Mercantile] and the Bank. Boarded train for Omena at 10:45, Mr. Stuart, conductor. Nice run! Mr. Kalchik met us and we dined at "The Oaks" with Miss Bevier, Mrs. Crabtree & Miss Wadsworth, Mrs. Parsons & family & Miss Walton. Mrs. Pierson met us at Camp L.

Fri., July 20, 1917
Pleasant. Mr. & Mrs. Vercoe delighted with the location. He brought a saw & axe & furnished wood for a cheerful fire tonight. Pretty well settled. Found both cottages all right. Called on neighbors Hibbard [Hibberd] & daughter Saxton. Mr. Sargent motored us over to his house, then with his family to Northport. Dinner at Oaks.

Sat., July 21, 1917
Pleasant. Very busy day. We took walk thru Woodland Way to Indian Garden then to Mr. Santo's for a call & at 2 p.m. Mr. Vercoe went to G.R. for Sunday services.

Sun., July 22, 1917
Hot all day but cool at evening. Mrs. Vercoe and I had morn. service under St. Andrew's tree. Dinner at The Oaks & visit with Miss Bevier & met Mrs. Rice & daugh., Mrs. Palmer. Reading on piazza this afternoon.

Mon., July 23, 1917
Quite hot day & evening. Mr. Vercoe returned at noon fr. G. Rapids. Wrote good letter to Sister Mary. Mrs. Hibbard [Hibberd] & Mrs. Saxton called this eve. ...

Tues., July 24, 1917
Hot & clear. Good work on paths & pruning. Dinner as usual at The Oaks; then nap, then sewing on piazza. Mrs. Pierson called. ... Bezique for 3 this eve.

Wed., July 25, 1917
Hot. Afternoon at Red Cross meeting at Mrs. Crabtree's. 28 women stripping & clipping cloth to fill ambulance pillows & Farrell Crabtree, collector. Letters fr. Mary K. [Kendall], Eliz. Custer. ...

Thurs., July 26, 1917
Very warm till evening. Mr. & Mrs. Pierson dined with us at Oaks, then we inspected their home & Morningside Terrace. Mr. Strahan of Northport spent part of the after-noon with us. Letter from Sister Mary.

Fri., July 2, 1917
Lovely Omena weather. Cool & sunny. Put up awnings at Bonnie B. & scattered gravel. P/c to E.L.C. Bezique this eve. by open fire: Mr. V. [Vercoe] won.

Sat., July 28, 1917
Cool, breezy morn. Fine for sweeping; at noon became hot & wind increased to a gale before night. We all sat on beach watching the breakers, then played Bezique.

Sun., July 29, 1917
Very high, hot wind. Mr. & Mrs. Hibbard [Hibberd] drove us to Northport Point to service in Bp. Atwill Memorial Chapel. Bp. McC. [McCormick] preaching a very fine sermon ... Wrote long letter to Mary K. Three on the beach this eve. Singing in moonlight.

Mon., July 30, 1917
Hot and quiet. Mr. Sargent called this morn. All glad to have the winds & waves stilled. Restless night, but slept finally in hammock today. Fixed a/c with Kalchik.

Wed., Aug. 1, 1917
Hot. The heat on N.Y., Chi, etc. has caused hundreds of prostrations & many dead. Mr. Leonard Wheeler died early this morn at Sunset Lodge: his brother was with him.

Thurs., Aug. 2, 1917
Cool: hearth fire acceptable. Mr. Vercoe did many last things for us today & left at 6 pm. for G. Rapids, having had 2 valuable weeks vacation. Mr. & Mrs. Hibbard [Hibberd] called. This morn. Mr. Vercoe had tennis at Sargents. ...

Fri., Aug. 3, 1917
A Perfect Omena Day!: sparkling air & water. Mrs. V. rode to Leland with the Hibbards. [Hibberds]...

Sat., Aug. 4, 1917
Cold in morn. Much warmer at mid-day, windy & threatening at eve. Looked in vain for Miss Yerkes. Guests of Mrs. Pierson & Mrs. Crabtree left.

Sun., Aug. 5, 1917
Beautiful Omena day. Morn. Service with Mrs.Vercoe. Mr. Kalchik took Miss Bevier & me to Mr. Wheeler's funeral this afternoon & Miss Ring brot [brought] us home. Cong. Ch. crowded & Rev. Mr. Rogers, Pres. conducted the services: "The new Life; the new Home; the new Song."

Tues., Aug. 7, 1917
Rain all night & all day. Sewing & writing. Mrs. Pierson called in afternoon & Mrs. Parsons & Mrs. Bent this eve. Rode with the Hibbards [Hibberds] to village & had notary execute papers wh. sent to Mary Kendall ...

Wed., Aug. 8, 1917
Rain all night & most of morn. Clear this afternoon. Mr. Sargent, wife & mother called this afternoon. We called at Log Cabin, Parsons & Bents this eve. & Hibbards [Hibberds].

Thurs., Aug 9, 1917
Rain in night & till 10 a.m. Settling Camp L. for leaving. Mrs. Vercoe left on 2 o'cl train after dining with Miss Yerkes who came at 12. Mrs. Rice & daugh. Mrs. Palmer called & we looked over old photos. Moved to The Oaks at noon.

Fri., Aug. 10, 1917
Cool & breezy. Miss Yerkes likes it here. Morn. at hotel writing, cottage this afternoon, Bezique this eve. Pd. by check hotel bill etc. for week ending 8th & sent dep. of $100 to Trav. City State Bk.

Sat., Aug. 11, 1917
Beautiful Omena day! ... Mrs. Dr. Munson of Traverse City brought Dr. & Mrs. Wilkinson & Helen, their daughter, in her car & we had a lovley visit.

Sun., Aug. 12, 1917
Rain this morn. Miss Yerkes wrote several letters. Sleep in hammock this afternoon. Later a call fr. Rev. & Mrs. Sargent & Rev. & Mrs. Torrence. Visit with Mrs. Pierson this eve.

Mon., Aug. 13, 1917
Heavy rain last night; hazy & threatening today. Miss Y. & I called at Pierson's, Spears', Palmer's, Crabtree's & Bevier's. She took the 2 p.m. train for Traverse, saying she enjoyed every moment here.

Pierson cottage, Pencroft

Tues., Aug. 14, 1917
Humid & hazy today but mild & good for work. Bigelow's men built me new stairs at Bonnie Banks ...

Wed., Aug. 15, 1917
Hazy & humid. Bigelow's men spent one and half days shingling at Camp L. I did small work at cottages ... Miss Rhodes took tea with me.

Thurs., Aug. 16, 1917
Cleaned up after men who did shingle small roof yes. morn, 2 men 1 & half days for small job.

Fri., Aug. 17, 1917
Calm & cold. Stephen boy & I spread fresh gravel on steps & walks. Wrote Emma C. that I should come home 24th. Comfortless evening at the hotel: no invitation next door!

Sat., Aug. 18, 1917
Rain. Half the day at cottage ... Spent the eve. with Mrs. Rellatti & Miss Rhodes played backgammon.

Tues., Aug. 21, 1917
Bright & warmer. Rode to Bonnie Banks this morn. & sorted hist. photos & showed them this eve. to Mrs. & Miss Torrence, Rev. & Mrs. Sargent (who took tea with me), Mr. & Mrs. Pierson & Miss Bevier. I am feeling miserable with my infected tooth & neuralgia.

Wed., Aug. 22, 1917
Hot & sultry. Rested this morn. & spent afternoon with Mrs. Kalchik closing cottages: Stevens helped. Very tired & sad! Miss B. [Bevier] & I took tea ... at the King cottage.

Thurs., Aug. 23, 1917
Humid & hazy: big thunderstorm bet. 2 and 4. Spent morn. at cottage doing last things. Boy helped finish & I pd. him 50 cents. Settled a/c with Geo. Anderson & gave him pictures & Omena photos. Eve. in backgammon with Miss Rhodes.

Fri., Aug. 24, 1917
Cold. Rain & wind. Signed checks for Bigelow the carpenter & Kalchik of The Oaks. Spent 2 hrs. in Miss Bevier's warm dining room. Brought dinner there over to cottages to cook & give keys to Kalchik. Found at station I was $3.00 short (?) Louis A. [Anderson] loaned me $2.00. Gave Con. Stuart [S.W.] picture & he helped me to vestibule car. Arrv. at 10. ...

1918

Tues., June 11, 1918
Warm & windy. Wrote S. Spillard & Susan Yerkes about summering. Anna Roberts called. Packed Omena trunk. ... Eve. with E.L.C. [Emma Chamberlain] backgammon.

Thurs., June 13, 1918
Cool & bright. Sent card to Geo. Anderson, 18th. Mr. Torrey called to see about Omena. Card to Mr. Santo. ...

Fri., June 14, 1918
June day all right. ... Good news fr. Sister Mary. Mr. Torrey called & we decided to go to Omena Monday: gave $6.00 for ticket. ...

Sat., June 15, 1918
Perfect June day, warm & breezy. Miss Roberts called & did errands for me. Miss Chamberlain went to Charlevoix today. I packing vigorously ... Carrie Lyon called & I gave her "The Hard Heart" by F.S.C. Gave Mrs. Noble Liberty Bd. [Bond] $5.00.

"The Hard Heart" by Frederick Stuart Church, Rebecca's cousin

Mon., June 17, 1918
Cool change in the night: so thankful! Closed rooms at noon. Kate Earle lunched with me: pd. Mrs. Noble to date. Started for Omena with Torreys & Kate E. [Earle] at 2:45. Supper & night at Hotel McKinnon. [Cadillac] Next morn. taxi around the lake & train at 11 for Traverse.

Tues., June 18, 1918
... Arriv. Omena at 3:30 ...

Wed., June 19, 1918
Clear & cool. After good breakfast prepared by Mrs. Torrey & Kate E. we began to put house & grounds in order.

Fri., June 21, 1918
Thunder-storm last night, putting rain water into our empty barrels.

Sat., June 22, 1918
Sharp cold & bright & breezy. Found a birthday present from the Torreys at the breakfast table: a great surprise!

Sun., June 23, 1918
Still real cold. ... Mr. & Mrs. Torrey rode to ch. with Geo. Anderson. 33 at dinner at The Oaks, Santos, Bradleys & Piersons ...

Tues., June 25, 1918
Milder! Thanks! Mr. T. [Torrey] and I worked along the walk. ... The Missouri passed us. Bezique this eve. Letters fr. San Jose & E.B.C. [Eliz. B. Custer]

Bay and Walk

Wed., June 26, 1918
All paid our week's board $5.25 apiece & 1 supper, 50 c. Mrs. Parsons of Log Cabin called. Bezique this eve. with Torreys. Mrs. T. won. Big storm tonight.

Thurs., June 27, 1918
South high wind after thunder-storm last night. Wrote Carrie Lyon in response to book sent me & card in answer to Calkins birthday greetings. The Torreys & I played Bezique, I won.

Sat., June 29, 1918
Mr. Torrey's 73rd birthday celebrated by little gifts fr. all & a "sonnet" fr. me.

Tues., July 2, 1918
Showery & cool. Mrs. Wanty & Mrs. Calkins arrived at 3:30.

Thurs., July 4, 1918
Cold & grey. Raising of service flag at Pres. Ch. this afternoon by 2 Indian boys: Rev. Rogers gave fine address: our ladies attended & Mr. T. went to ball game later. Rain tonight.

Sat., July 6, 1918
High wind but mild. Mrs. Wanty treated us to a ride to Northport Point; inspected the rustic ch. dedicated to the memory of Bp. Atwill of Kansas City by his sons.

Sun., July 7, 1918
Cool & sunny. To Pres. Ch. went Mr. & Mrs. T., Mrs. W. [Wanty] & Mrs. Calkins. 30 people at dinner at The Oaks. ... Walked to Indian Garden. Prof. Slocum & family called fr. Cinn.

Mon., July 8, 1918
Warmer & sunny & still. An Omena day. Mr. & Mrs. Hibbard [Hibberd] took Mrs. Wanty, Calkins & Torrey to Leland this afternoon. ... Mrs. W. at tea at Mrs. Santo's.

Wed., July 10, 1918
Mrs. Wanty left on the 9 a.m. train, having been here just a week.

Thurs., July11, 1918
Mrs. Collins Johnston and daugh. Caroline dined with us.

Wed., July 17, 1918
Pleasant. Mrs. Calkins returned to G.R. by the 9 a.m. train. We all called at the Pierson's this eve. and Mrs. Johnston, in the moonlight.

Thurs., July 18, 1918
Bright & breezy. Rev. and Mrs. Rogers dined with us today; they have the Pres. Mission to the Indians here in hand for 5 years. Fine people – she born in Niles, her father a pioneer banker.

Sat., July 20, 1918
... Mr. Hibbard's [Hibberd's] new pier was finished today & the neighbors sat on the long bench & enjoyed the sunset & moonlight. Pd. plumber's bill $6.15.

"Omena" Pullman car of the G.R. & I. Railway

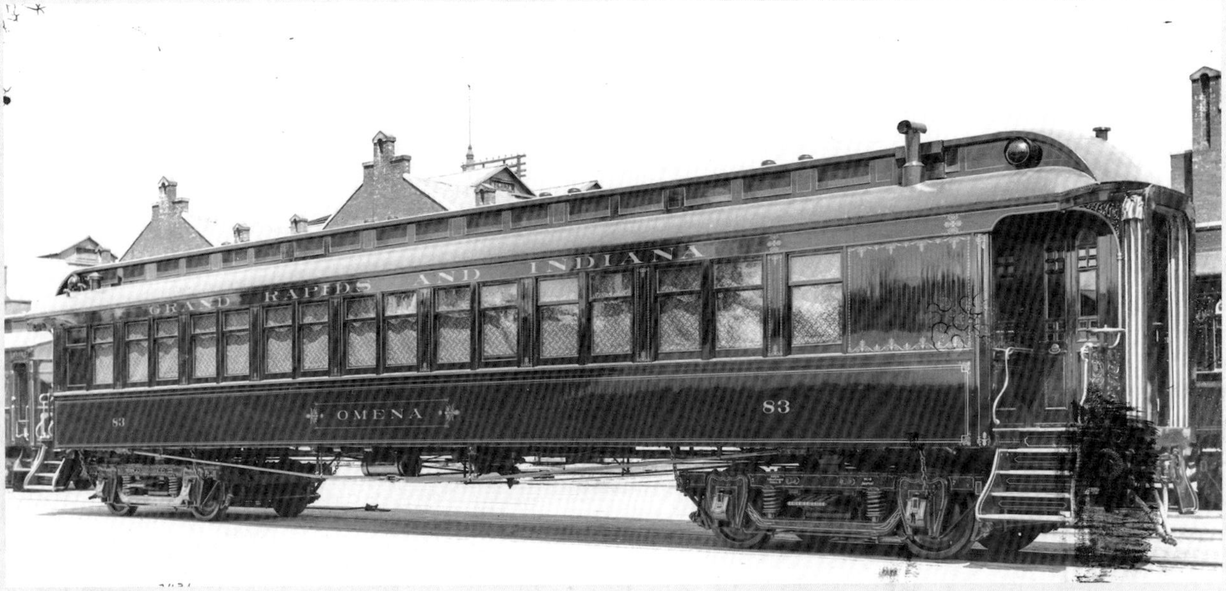

Sun., July 21, 1918
Hot! 48 persons at "The Oaks" dinner today. News rec'd of the death of Ex-Pres. Roosevelt's son by an airplane wh. fell in the German lines.

Tues., July 30, 1918
Cool & bright. Busy day for Kate E. [Earle] and me closing Bonnie Banks and paying bills. Last dinner at The Oaks, and at 4:30 the Hibbards [Hibberds] took us to station in their car, Stuart [S.W.] treated us in "Pullman." Supped at "Sam's" at Traverse, then to Park Hotel, welcomed by Holden ...

Wed., July 31, 1918
Crisp, cool, furnace heat in hotel. Mildred gave us fine breakfast: took Mr. Anderson's [John H.] train at 10:30, G.R. car joining Mackinac train at Walton, & arrived in G.R. at 4:30 p.m. E.L.C. arr. yesterday & greeted me on the piazza of Elmwood. Rooms in order & Mrs. Noble with welcome. Glad to be home. Torreys arr. at 9 p.m. having left Omena at 9 a.m. & Trav. C. at 3 p.m.

Motoring on country road

Sun., Aug. 18, 1918
... Ry. fr. Traverse City – Northport discontinued: panic among resorters. [was reinstated later]. Mercury rose to 78 degrees at evening.

Wed., Aug. 28, 1918
Wrote Omena for Deview's report. 4 things achieved? Four weeks today arrived from Omena. Pd. Mrs. Noble mine & 9 guests, $34.40. ... Called on Wanty's this eve. just returned fr. 3 wks. at Omena. Ry. closed & they had to motor to Traverse City. ...

Fri., Aug. 30, 1918
Cool. ... Letter fr. Louis Anderson reporting shingling & painting and repairing porch by Deview. Wrote Sister Mary & p/c. to Miss Yerkes. First good rain in 2 mos. tonight.

Mon., Sept. 2, 1918 - Labor Day
... Wrote Louis Anderson enclosing check for $20 for Ed Deview & list of things he is to do on my land as caretaker.

1919

Sat., May 31, 1919
… [Letter] fr. Louis Anderson, saying "The Oaks" would likely open on the 10th & Ry service sometime.

Mon., June 23, 1919
Cool & breezy; Very glad! … This eve. on Mrs. Johnston's piazza. Mrs. Pierson in the hospital, delayed going to Omena.

Wed., June 25, 1919
Cool morning, showers. Very hot & humid this afternoon. Packed jellies etc. to go North. Miss Orth bro't [brought] 40 copies of Omena hymns she has made for me. She regrets being unable to go to Omena.

Fri., June 27, 1919
Sad letter from Mrs. Wilkinson, sick & can't go to Omena. The Hibbards [Hibberds] passed thru en route to Omena. Mr. & Mrs. Torrey called this eve. Bringing cherries. …

Hymn to Omena.

Composed by
Miss Richmond
and
Mrs. Willard.

Omena, the gem of creation,
The home of the evergreen tree,
The shrine of the tourist's devotion
We offer our homage to thee.
May thy lovers, united, ne'er falter,
But e'er to thy forests prove true;
Omena, we're thine, now and ever—
Three cheers for thy waters so blue.

O the sail-boat, the sail-boat, "The Viking,"
With Peterson firm at the helm,
For thee we'll forsake even biking,
To roam over Neptune's broad realm.
We will mount every high, foaming billow
That rises with feathery crest,
Or we'll float o'er thy calm, gentle wavelets,
With our oars and our cares all at rest.

O "beautiful gift," fair Omena,
To the winds we thy colors unfold,
The green for thy blossoming spring-time,
For thy autumn, the crimson and gold.
We will sing of Omena the glorious,
Every year brings new joys to our view;
Omena, Omena, victorious!
Three cheers for thy waters so blue!

Chorus—

Three cheers for thy waters so blue,
Three cheers for thy waters so blue,
Omena, Omena, victorious,
Three cheers for thy waters so blue!

The Omena Yell.

Hobble gobble, razzle dazzle,
Zip, boom, bah!
Omena, Omena, rah, rah, rah!

Omena Colors.

Crimson, green and gold.

Rev. Dr. Anna Howard Shaw

Sat., July 5, 1919
Dr. Anna Howard Shaw died Wed., July 2, aged 71. Funeral for Anna Shaw, famed suffragist, with great honors. Youth spent near Big Rapids, Mich. ...

Tues., July 8, 1919
Delightfully cool this morn. & a breeze kept it fr. being oppressive later. Rec'd letter from Nell Bevier inviting me to share her house if friends were delayed, to which I replied at once with thanks. ...

Fri., July 11, 1919
Delightfully cool. Morn. at papers & figures. ... Vercoes called this eve. to arrange for Omena ...

Sat., July 12, 1919
Cool morn. & evening, hot & humid mid-day. Fussing over preparations for Omena. Wrote & mailed to Mrs. Hibbard [Hibberd], Ed Deview & Louis Anderson, Omena telling of Thurs. plan. Mrs. Corsont sent good cheer fr. Omena.

Union Station, Grand Rapids

Mon., July 14, 1919
Hot & humid. Sent box of jellies etc. [from Grand Rapids] to Louis Anderson, Omena, for Camp Lookout by ex [express]: also wrote him & Park Hotel engaging 3 rooms for Wed. night. Began packing trunk. Rain after 6 and cooler. ...

Tues., July 15, 1919
Delightfully cool after 8 a.m.: breeze all day. Thanks! Very busy getting ready for trip to Omena. ...

Wed., July 16, 1919
Fine! Finished packing & closing rooms & after lunch met Mr. & Mrs. Vercoe & son Harry from overseas at the Union Station at 2:30 & off for Traverse City; good trip in Pullman, met old friend Anderson & arr. at Park Place Hotel & fine bed at 8:30. ...

Thurs., July 17, 1919
Beautiful, cool, bright day. Off for Omena at 10:30 on Ry. under new management. Arr. Omena at 11:30. At The Oaks for dinner at 12:30 meeting Bevier, Piersons, Crabtrees & Mrs. Spear & Miss Ring. Our good neighbors the Hibbards [Hibberds] are here & the log cabin people, Parsons & nieces. Letter to E.L.C. [Emma Chamberlain]

Fri., July 18, 1919
Another beautiful day. Opened Bonnie Banks: all right. Mrs. Hibbard [Hibberd] & Mrs. Deview opened & settled Camp Lookout yesterday morn., kindly welcoming us: very acceptable!

Sat., July 19, 1919
Hot. Mr. Vercoe took the noon train for Traverse City & Elk Rapids. I sent letter to Kate Earle. Package fr. E.L.C.

Sun., July 20, 1919
Pretty warm & bright. Mrs. V. [Vercoe] and I had morn. service on the piazza. Mrs. Hibbard's [Hibberd's] maid being gone, I invited her, her husband & Betty to dine with us on their return fr. Ch. at Northport where Mr. Bradley preached.

Mon., July 21, 1919
Still, warm night, many variations today: hazy & warm - sharp showers at noon: cool change & breezy later. Inspected Sunnyside [Rood cottage] after dinner. No newspapers fr. home yet.

C.F. Rood cottage, Sunnyside

Tues., July 22, 1919
Lovely quiet June day. Fine ride with Hibbards [Hibberds] to the Lookout, beyond Northport. Mrs. V. & Harry boated this eve. ...

Thurs., July 24, 1919
Pd. "The Oaks" for one week. Perfect summer day. Mrs. Pierson escorted Mrs. V. & H. [son Harry] to Heart's Ease this morn. This eve. the last 2 went to the community dance with Mrs. & Miss VanBoren. Destructive fires on Little Traverse Bay route & the Manistee River. ...

Fri., July 25, 1919
Showery, ending in electric storm at eve. while Mrs. V. and I were playing Bezique; I one game, she one, then side by side in the third till last lap when she got 500 and sped far away to 1300! Parlor maid swept upper floor. ...

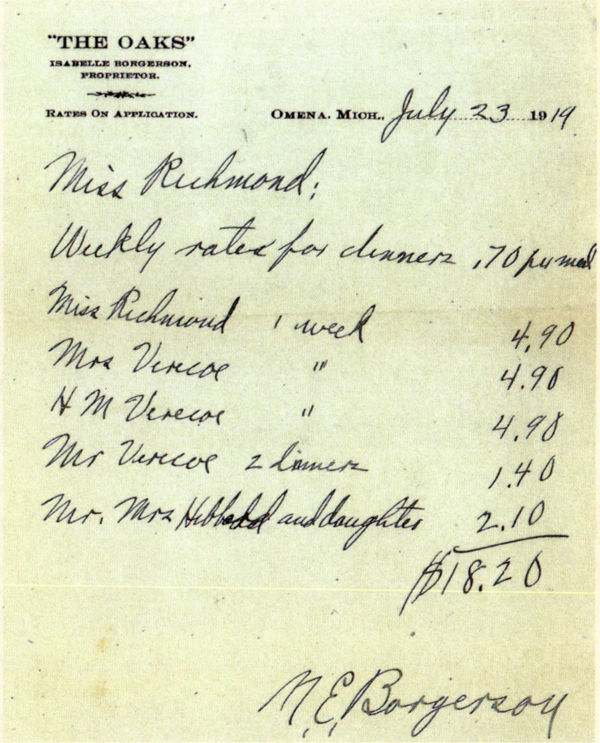
"THE OAKS"
ISABELLE BORGERSON,
PROPRIETOR.

RATES ON APPLICATION. OMENA. MICH., July 23 1919

Miss Richmond;

Weekly rates for dinner .70 per meal

Miss Richmond	1 week	4.90
Mrs Vercoe	"	4.90
H M Vercoe	"	4.90
Mr Vercoe	2 dinner	1.40
Mr. Mrs Hibbard and daughter		2.10
		$18.20

M. E. Borgerson

Sat., July 26, 1919
Electric storm all night & till 10 this morn. Parlor swept this morn. Introduced to some nice newcomers at Oaks, Mrs. Schuyler of Chi, Mrs. & Miss VanBehren of Marion, Ind. Mrs. V. and I called on Miss Bevier & the Piersons. First G.R. papers today. High winds in eve. & in night.

Sun., July 27, 1919
Pleasant morn, but high wind. Nice walk to dinner at 12:30, then hurried home on a/c of gathering electric storm that lasted all afternoon.

Tues., July 29, 1919
Calm & bright & all right. Finished putting Bonnie Banks in order. Wrote Miss Kate Johnson this aftern. inviting her to come as she suggests - also to Ch. Mission pledging $125 for benefit. ...

Wed., July 30, 1919
Fog, and cool. Misses Bevier & Alyce Twanley arrived at the Oaks fr. G.R. this p.m. - their cousin Fred will follow later.

Thurs., July 31, 1919
Cool & clear. Fire on the hearth by which the Twanleys visited this morning & Mrs. Schuyler & Mrs. Byford this afternoon. Wrote Mrs. Wilkinson and Mrs. Burford. Pd. "The Oaks" for 1 week for 3 persons, 1 meal per day, $14.

Sat., Aug. 2, 1919
Cool & bright & breezy. Wrote to Cousin Mary Church, N. Befdord. Capt. Harry returned this p.m. from Traverse, where he visited the Sanders.

Sun., Aug. 3, 1919
Grey & threatening but not cold: fire on hearth this eve. Wrote to Kate Johnson & Emma L.C. ...

Tues., Aug. 5, 1919
Good clearance day in my attic at Bonnie B. Fire last night at Crabtree cottage made panic along Morningside & at The Oaks. ...

Crabtree cottage

Wed., Aug. 6, 1919
Warmer & sunny. Mrs. Schuyler & Mrs. Byford spent forenoon at Bonnie Banks. Wrote Elizabeth Custer. Collecting rummage fr. Bonnie Banks for Rev. Rogers' work.

Thurs., Aug. 7, 1919
Pd. week board and laundry $15.45. Dubious weather, hazy & windy. Fussing at Bonnie Banks.

Fri., Aug. 8, 1919
Cold & breezy. Sweeping morn. .... Playlet by Mrs. Pierson & acted by 4 children in Hibbard [Hibberd] woods this afternoon. I gave souvenirs. Fine, cool, bright day.

Sat., Aug. 9, 1919
Cool & hazy. ... Busy at Bonnie Banks rummaging. This eve. calls fr. Mr. & Mrs. Pierson, Three Foot sisters from Cinn.. and Mrs. Hibbard [Hibberd].

Bonnie Banks

Presbyterian Manse

Sun., Aug. 10, 1919
Andrew Carnegie dies, is to be buried at Tarrytown. Pretty warm! Must be hot in the cities. No services today out here. Fred & Bessie T. called at Bonnie Banks. Mr. & Mrs. Angell called en route fr. Northport to T.C. ...

Mon., Aug. 11, 1919
Fine day! Busy with Mr. Deview, painting, etc. Mrs. Vercoe & Alyce Twamley are my guests joined by Mrs. Pierson & Mrs. Wicks in trip to Lighthouse Pt. ...

Tues., Aug. 12, 1919
Quite warm day, cool more at eve. Working hard at Bonnie Banks. Wrote cards to Park Hotel, the T.C. Bank, and Carrie Lyon. Rode with Mr. & Mrs. Hibbard [Hibberd] after tea to call at the Manse & Mrs. Rogers to deliver articles for Ch. Bazaar. ...

Wed., Aug. 13, 1919
Hazy & cool. Rain afternoon. Pd. Northport & Scott to date. Hurrying to close Bonnie Banks. Bid adieu to friends at hotel. Mr. & Mrs. Paul Sargent called this morn., having welcomed the Torrance women just arrived at The Oaks.

Thurs., Aug. 14, 1919 - Traverse City
Cool & bright. Deview helped us close Camp L. & I gave keys to Mrs. Hibbard [Hibberd]. At 11:30 Mr. H. [Hibberd] motored us to station. Pd. Hotel bill & sent laundry to be delivered to Mrs. Hibbard [Hibberd]. Pd. Deview & Kalchik. Arr'd Trav. City at 1 o'cl. Mrs. Angell took us to Hotel for lunch after wh. Mrs. V. [Vercoe] & I went to Bank: She & Harry dined at Sanders & I rode with Mrs. Angell, Mrs. Morgan & Mrs. Cameron.

Fri., Aug. 15, 1919
Cool, overcast & showery. Mrs. V. & I breakfasted alone. G.R. & I. at 10:30. John H. Anderson conducting us to Walton Junc., where [we] wait 1:30 train. Arr'd G.R. 5:30, met by Mr. V. and son, & I at Elmwood by ever-attentive E.L.C. Rooms cleaned & in order.

Thurs., Aug. 21, 1919
... An awful wreck on Pere Marquette Ry. Near Traverse City yesterday morn, 6 dead & 17 injured.

1920

Sat., May 15, 1920 - Grand Rapids
.... From G.H. [Grand Haven] came Miss Hatfield to rent Camp Lookout for the summer fr. June 8. Then I wrote to Mrs. Wilkinson who had applied for friends; and Louis Anderson about keys & Kalchik. ...

Mon., June 7, 1920
... Miss Hatfield called & I sent her by taxi to station for Traverse City where she expects to meet sister fr. Boston & then to Omena tomorrow. ...

Thurs., June 10, 1920
P.C. from Miss Hatfield announcing their safe arrival at Omena. ...

Fri., June 25, 1920
Letter fr ... Miss Hatfield saying they were very happy at Camp Lookout. ...

Fri., Aug. 6, 1919
... Papers fr. Libbie Custer about Custer Nat. Park in Montana & big dam on Bighorn River.

Gravestone at Custer National Monument

FRONT STREET, LOOKING EAST, TRAVERSE CITY, MICH.

Fri., Aug. 27, 1920
Pleasant. Very busy packing & closing. ... Mr. Bird took us to station at 4 o'cl. for G.R. & I. train: checked suitcases. John Anderson met us at Walton, arr. Trav. at 9 o'cl, Park Pl. for much needed rest.

Sat., Aug. 28, 1920
Lovely morn. Good sleep & breakfast. Downtown for stroll. Left checkbook & $50 deposit at State Bank with Miss Sherwood. Then called on Mr. Santo. Lunch at hotel with Mr. Holden & Margaret. ... Train for Omena at 4:30. Met the Barnabys going to the Clovers. Kalchik's Ford took us to "The Oaks" for supper. Misses Aylesworth, hostesses.

Sun., Aug. 29, 1920
Pleasant morn. Mild & sunny but wet afternoon. Mrs. B. [Baker] and I walked over to cottages this morn & found all right but orphaned, all Omena looks that way, dejected. Called on Mrs. Spear & Miss Ring, their cottage sold to Mrs. Pierson! Music in parlor this eve. ...

Mon., Aug. 30, 1920
Morn. dedicated to settling. Afternoon regulated superficially Bonnie Banks, looked into trunk, etc. We met very nice people this year ... Mrs. Smith (slender) of Chi., Mrs. Fish (corpulent) of Wheaton, Ill., Mrs. Pierson, the Russells. Crabtrees, etc. The new Carmichael cottage is occupied.

Tues., Aug. 31, 1920
Partly sunny but cold & damp from rain last night. Called on Mrs. Parsons at the Log Cabin where she is alone this year, then over to cottages for regulating a bit. Rest this afternoon & greeted Edna Spillard & Sara Crane at 6 o'cl fr. Charlevoix. ...

Wed., Sept. 1, 1920
Bright all day, quite Omena weather! My guests hiked over to Ingalls Bay this morn. & I saw Rev. & Mrs. Bradley. ... All went to Bonnie Banks this afternoon & joyously inspected. Found all O.K. and guests pleased. Quiet eve. by fire & early to bed.

Thurs., Sept. 2, 1920
Sunny & cool. Mrs. Baker & Mrs. Crane walked to the village. Edna took the hammock and I the pen. Afternoon gave fine drive in Mr. Santo's car to Sargents etc.

Fri., Sept. 3, 1920
Pleasant still. Guests called at Mrs. Pierson's to look at Spear cottage for possible rent by Mrs. Grace of Detroit. Found guitar in cleaning "secret chamber" & took it to The Oaks where we had jolly music by the open fire in the eve., Edna playing. Dr. Druke & family left in their car this morn. for Chi.

Sat., Sept. 4, 1920
Pleasant. Cinn. guests off this morn. Mrs. B. & I went to the cottages for a while this afternoon.

Spear cottage

Sun., Sept. 5, 1920
Very quiet morn. on the upper balcony of the hotel. At cottages this afternoon sorting keys, separating C.L. from B.B. Mr. Santo called about A.T.P.'s [Abel T. Page] lots & trees. Mrs. Fish played sacred music in parlor tonight.

Mon., Sept. 6, 1920
Signs of rain, as we went to cottages this morn. to finish up. ...

Tues., Sept. 7, 1920
Bright morn. & mild day. Left Oaks at 8:30, Mrs. Fish of Wheaton only boarder left. Rec'd bills fr. Aylesworth & Kalchik, pay at home. Met John Anderson at Traverse as usual. Comfortable ride down to G.R. where good Mr. Sargent of Grace Ch. met us with his car! Mrs. Sargent called this eve. Mrs. Baker dined with me. ...

Fri., Sept. 10, 1920
Grey morn, sun in p.m. Slept most of morn. ... Sent checks to The Oaks & to Kalchik.

Sun., Sept. 12, 1920
I am home fr. Omena in good shape. ...

Rebecca Richmond at her beloved Omena

Name Glossary from Rebecca Richmond Diaries

Akeley Hall/Institute - In 1888 Mr. Healy C. Akeley donated the Akeley mansion to the Episcopal Diocese of Western Michigan to be used as a facility to educate young women. The institute grew to be ranked with the leading schools in the West. This reputation allowed it to acquire a nationally representative corps of students. Though primarily a finishing school, it had a special curriculum for entrance to the University of Michigan. Since most of the faculty was from the finest eastern colleges, the girls were presented with an opportunity for certifying their admission to those schools also. The last graduating class was in 1928.

Anderson, Frank J. - Son of Andrew and Maret Anderson. He and his brother Louis spearheaded building the Omena Pavilion.

Anderson, John H. - Brakeman on the G.R. & I. Railroad.

Anderson, Louis E. - Son of Andrew and Maret Anderson. He bought the Anderson store from his father about 1928-29. He had been the Omena postmaster from 1914-1929, and served in the Michigan House of Representatives, 1951-52. He and his brother Frank spearheaded building the Omena Pavilion. Louis later moved to Northport and opened a store there. He died in 1954.

Atwill, Rev. Edward - Bishop of the Diocese of Kansas City. He first conducted religious services at the Cedar Lodge in Northport. In 1905 he came to stay at Northport Point, and, after his death in 1911, a small log chapel was built in his honor, the Atwill Memorial Chapel.

Baker, Ellen L. - Mrs. Baker was the widow of Henry P. Baker, and a Grand Rapids friend of Rebecca, who visited Omena several times. She lived to the age of 101.

Barth, Paul & Christina Alpers Barth - Paul Barth operated the P.R. Barth General Merchandise store, one of two general stores in Omena operating during Rebecca's time there.

Bevier, Mary & Nell [Cornelia] - The two sisters built a cottage, "Wilder-Dee" at the Point about 1897. They lived in Grand Rapids where their father was one of the early physicians in town. Mary died in 1910. Nell became a close friend of Rebecca, and spent time with her both in Grand Rapids and Omena. Nell, for the last 15 years of her life, lived in Stanton, Michigan where she died in 1936.

Bradley, Rev. Dr. Dan Freeman - Received his doctorate in theology from Oberlin Theological Seminary in 1885. Rebecca likely met him when he was a pastor at Park Congregational Church in Grand Rapids from 1892-1902. During that period he built one of the earliest cottages at Omena called Cedarmere, which later became the Oaks Hotel. With two other appointments to serve outside of Michigan, he left Omena behind for several years before returning. He died in 1939.

Chamberlain, Emma L. - Miss Chamberlain had the apartment next door to Rebecca Richmond at the Elmwood in Grand Rapids. She and Rebecca spent much time together in Grand Rapids, and Emma occasionally visited Rebecca in Omena.

Church, Frederick Stuart - Born in GR in 1842, he was a second cousin to Rebecca Richmond. (Their grandmothers were sisters.) He studied at the National Academy of Design and then established his studio in New York City. He achieved fame as a painter of animals, and was well-known for his book and magazine illustrations. He and Rebecca corresponded regularly, sometimes sending her drawings. Rebecca donated some of his work for an exhibit at the Grand Rapids Art Association. She also donated several works to the Grand Rapids Public Library.

Currier, Prof. Arthur H. & Mrs. Ellen B. - Of Oberlin College in Ohio. They built a cottage on The Point about 1897.

Custer, Elizabeth (Libbie) Bacon - Libbie was a cousin to Rebecca Richmond. Her father was Judge Daniel Bacon and her mother was Eleanor Page Bacon, sister to Rebecca's mother, Loraine Page Richmond. After Libbie's mother died in 1854, Libbie stayed with her aunt Loraine for a while and grew close to her cousins Rebecca and Mary Richmond. She married George Armstrong Custer in 1864. Libbie inherited property in Omena from her father, Judge Daniel Bacon. It is conjectured that the Custers may have traveled to Omena, but no positive proof has been found. Libbie and Rebecca corresponded frequently, and she did visit Rebecca in Grand Rapids.

Cutcheon, General Byron M. - He served in the Civil War where he was promoted to Brigadier General before he resigned from the military service in 1865. He was awarded the Congres-sional Medal of Honor in 1891. He lived in Manistee, Michigan where he served in various prominent positions before being elected to the U.S. Congress in 1882, where he served for nine years. He and his wife then moved to Grand Rapids where he practiced law, worked as an editor for the *Detroit Daily Tribune* and the *Detroit Journal*, and wrote books relating to Michigan history. Byron & Marie Cutcheon built their cottage at Omena, the Maplewood, about 1896 or 1897. The Cutcheons probably made the Omena connection through Rev. Dan Bradley, pastor of Park Congregational Church in Grand Rapids.

Cutcheon, Marie (Mrs. B.M. Cutcheon) - Marie A. Warner married General B.M. Cutcheon in 1863, in the midst of the Civil War. They first settled in Manistee, Michigan, then later in Washington D.C., eventually moving to Grand Rapids.

Cutcheon, Max Hart - Son of General Byron Cutcheon, and likely inherited his father's cottage after his death in 1908.

Deview, Edward - He became Rebecca Richmond's handyman and property manager in 1911.

Earle, Emma & Kate M. - Sisters of Lawrence C. Earle, a distinguished water-color artist of national fame. Both sisters lived in Grand Rapids in the early part of the 20th century and visited Rebecca at Omena.

Eagles, Nancy Aunt (NRE) - Rebecca's aunt who lived in Auburn, New York, where Rebecca visited her in June of 1914. Graves, Frank H. & Frances - Frank Graves of Grand Rapids, bought 151 acres of property on Omena Point in 1892. It was surveyed and platted in 1893 and named the Plat of New Mission Point on Omena Bay. The Omena Inn was near the east end of the plat. Partnering with Abel T. Page, the two men promoted the Omena Bay Resort, publishing promotional booklets starting in 1898.

Greene Brothers - William O. & Fred A. started a surveying business in 1890 and were hired by Frank H. Graves in 1893 to plat the land for Omena Point.

Grierson, Benjamin H., - Of Jacksonville, Illinois. He was a Union cavalry officer in the Civil War, but promoted to Brigadier General in 1863. He built a cottage in Omena in 1896, naming it "The Garrison." He also bought other property at Omena, including the Oaks Hotel.

Lillian King Grierson - Second wife of Benjamin Grierson. They were married in 1897.

Hibbard [Hibberd], Edgar G. & Elizabeth - The family was from Richmond, Indiana, their son was Wilbur. They were cottage neighbors to Rebecca.

Holden, William O. - Manager of the Park Place Hotel at the time Rebecca stayed there while in Traverse City.

Kalchik, Joseph C. - Was "jack-of-all-trades" and often met resorters at the train station or the docks, escorting them to their destination, and offering other cottage services. In 1913 he purchased the Oaks Hotel, which many people on the Point, including Rebecca Richmond, depended on for meals and occasional overnight accommodations.

Kendall, Mary Elizabeth (Mrs. Charles F. Kendall) - Rebecca's younger sister. She married Charles Freeman Kendall, a merchant and real estate broker from Kalamazoo in 1867. They settled in Kansas and had two children who both died about the age of two. Before she moved to Hollywood, California, Mary had often visited Rebecca in Omena. Mary died in 1918 and left the income from the residuals of her estate to be paid to Rebecca in her lifetime, after which the principal is to be divided equally between Butterworth Hospital in Grand Rapids and the Home for Aged Women in Topeka, Kansas.

Lyon, Carrie M. - Widow of Farnham Lyon. She knew Rebecca through St. Mark's Church in Grand Rapids. Like Rebecca, she was prominent in the early social life of the city. She died in 1929.

Mrs. Annie McBride (Mrs. James G. McBride) [MacBride] - Wife of James G. McBride

James G. McBride. [MacBride] - Served under Custer in the Civil War. Married to Annie Perkins.

Josephine McBride. [MacBride] - Daughter of Annie & James G. McBride.
McCormick, John, Newton - Was appointed rector of St. Mark's Episcopal Church in Grand Rapids in 1898. He then served as rector of churches in Virginia and Georgia, before being appointed as Bishop of the Episcopal Diocese of Western Michigan.

McCormick, Bessie Chapman Tucker - Wife of John N. McCormick. She died in 1938.

Noble. Mrs. - Rebecca's landlady of the Elmwood in Grand Rapids.

Page, Abel Town - Rebecca's uncle became interested in Omena in 1890 and purchased 70 acres on Omena Bay. In1891 he bought his brother Aaron's home, and turned it into a summer resort, calling it "Che-Min-Wah-Be." He and Frank Graves, both from Grand Rapids, promoted Omena and sold lots to the resort. They built the first Omena Inn in 1896.

Parsons, Mary (Mrs. James A.) - In 1910 Mary Parsons and her sister Josephine, Mrs. Henry Bents, bought a log cabin in Omena. Like several other Omena resorters, Mary was from Jacksonville, Illinois.

Peck, Alphonso - Worker on the Grand Rapids & Indiana Railroad.

Pierson, Clara Dillingham - Born in 1868 in Coldwater, Michigan. She taught a two-year training course at Alma College before her marriage to John W.S. Pierson in 1894. After her marriage she began writing books for and about children. Her nature books were especially popular, including *Among the Meadow People* (1897), *Among the Forest People* (1898), *Among the Pond People* (1901), and others. Clara and John built a cottage at Omena Point in 1897, and named it "Pencroft" since it was built using the money Clara earned from her pen. Clara wrote a series of four "Pencroft" books which were based on a fictional family living in the area. Clara lived most of her life in Stanton, Michigan, but settled in Grand Rapids in her later years. She and Rebecca were quite good friends, and Clara visited her in Grand Rapids.

Pollard, Annie Archer - Assistant librarian at the Grand Rapids Public Library. She was interested in historical research and preservation of historical spots in Kent County. She also was active with the American Library Assoc. in providing reading material to American soldiers in WW I. Rebecca dealt with Miss Pollard when donating material to the library. They became friends and Miss Pollard stayed at Camp Lookout in Omena. She died in 1958.

Richmond, Charles H. (wife, Willa S. Richmond) - Cousin of Rebecca. Formerly lived in Grand Rapids, then Philadelphia and later Los Angeles, California.

Richmond, Mary A. - Sister of Charles H. Richmond, and cousin of Rebecca. Both brother and sister visited Rebecca in Omena in 1908. In later life she lived in La Jolla, California.

Rood, Charles F. & Harriet C. - Owned "Sunnyside" cottage at Omena Point.

Santo, John R. & Frances Santo - John sold insurance from an office in Traverse City and, starting in 1899, invested in real estate in Omena. He served as the Mayor of Traverse City in 1903. Santo built five cottages not far from Rebecca's cottages on the east shore of Omena Bay.

Sargent, Rev. George P.T. & wife Mabel - He was rector, Grace Episodical Church, Grand Rapids.

Spear, Mary A. - From Oberlin, Ohio. She built a cottage on The Point a few years after Rebecca Richmond built Bonnie Banks.

Spillard, Edna - A close friend of Rebecca's, she inherited Bonnie Banks upon Rebecca's death in 1925, and owned it until the 1940s.

Stuart, S.W. - A conductor on the Grand Rapids & Indiana Railroad.

Torrey, Arthur C. (wife Kate S.) - Grand Rapids friends who traveled with Rebecca from Grand Rapids to Omena on several occasions.

Torrey, Kate S. (Mrs. Arthur C.) - Grand Rapids friend of Rebecca's who visited frequently at Rebecca's home in Grand Rapids and in Omena. She was a trained artist with education at the Art Institute of Chicago, as well as schools in New York and in Europe.

Townsend, Emilie - Was a teacher in Grand Rapids public schools and at Western State Normal School [later became University of West Michigan]. She died in 1966 at the Isabella Home for Aged Women, which Rebecca Richmond had supported.

Vercoe, Lincoln Russell, Rev. - Rector St. Paul's Memorial Episcopal Church in Grand Rapids, then at Trinity Episcopal Church in Grand Ledge, before becoming assistant Rector at St. Mark's Episcopal Church, where Rebecca was a member. He later was appointed Archdeacon.

Vercoe, Eugenie Mary, (Mrs. Lincoln R.) - Knew Rebecca from St. Marks's Church.

Wheeler, Leonard H. and Rhoda Spicer Wheeler - Owners of Sunset Lodge.

Wheeler, Rhoda - Niece of Rhoda and Leonard Wheeler, owners of Sunset Lodge.

Willard, Eleanor - Grand Rapids resident, who bought property for a cottage on The Point in 1896. She may have known Rebecca through art circles and women's clubs in Grand Rapids. She was a photographer and lecturer on art history.

Wilkinson, Elizabeth (Mrs. James E.) - Served with Rebecca on the Women's Auxillary of the Protestant Diocese of Western Michigan. Her daughters were Helen and Mary. They frequently visited Rebecca in Omena.

Yerkes, Susan - Susan and her sister, Mary Yerkes, were co-principals at Akeley Hall in Grand Haven beginning in 1901, when Rev. and Mrs. Wilkinson retired. Susan was a Latin teacher. Under the sisters' direction, Akeley Hall became notable for its culture and advanced education. Susan visited Rebecca both at Omena and in Grand Rapids. She died in 1937.

Illustration Credits & Sources

With much gratitude to the following institutions and individuals for allowing use of their images.

Front Cover: *Omena Resort*, [1903], Library of Michigan;
viii. Omena Historical Society and Rob Burdick; **1.** Grand Rapids History Center, Grand Rapids Public Library; 2. Civil War Talk, https://civilwartalk.com/threads/george-armstrong-custer-photos-8-of-12.127455/; **3.** Grand Rapids History Center, Grand Rapids Public Library; **6.** City of Grand Rapids Community Archives & Research Center; **7-8.** Grand Rapids History Center, Grand Rapids Public Library; **9**. *Omena Resort*, [1901], Bentley Historical Library, University of Michigan; **10.** upper, Leelanau Historical Society; **11.** Grand Rapids History Center, Grand Rapids Public Library; **13.** Buehler Family Collection; **14.** Jill Cheney; **15.** Jim Winslow Sr.; **22.** Leelanau Historical Society; **23.** NPR, courtesy of Doug Seroff; **25.** Omena Historical Society; **28**. Traverse Area District Library; **30**. Leelanau Historical Society; **32.** Buehler Family Collection; **35.** Wally Jung; **41.** Bentley Historical Library, University of Michigan; **44-45.** Omena Historical Society; **46.** Leelanau Historical Society; **47.** Bentley Historical Library, University of Michigan; **49.** Leelanau Historical Society; **51.** Jill Cheney; **54.** Centurian Photos, Mark Worrall; **59.** Bentley Historical Library, University of Michigan; **61.** left, *West Michigan Pike Guide,* 1914; **62.** left, Omena Historical Society; **64.** *Omena Resort*, [1903], Library of Michigan; **65.** *Omena Resort*, [1901], Bentley Historical Library, University of Michigan; **68-69**. Bentley Historical Library, University of Michigan; 77. Leelanau Historical Society; **86**. Lynn Contos; **88**. Centurian Photos, Mark Worrall; **91**. Library of Congress; **93.** Leelanau Historical Society; **96.** Bentley Historical Library, University of Michigan; **97.** Carnegie Museum of Art; **99.** Leelanau Historical Society; **100.** Lynn Contos; **103.** Jim Winslow, Sr.; **105.** *Omena Resort*, [1901], Bentley Historical Library, University of Michigan; **106.** Archives of Michigan; **107.** Grand Rapids History Center, Grand Rapids Public Library; **108.** *Omena Resort* [1901], Bentley Historical Library, University of Michigan; **109.** Buehler Family Collection; **111.** Omena Historical Society; **112.** *Omena Resort*, [1901], Bentley Historical Library, University of Michigan; **113.** Omena Historical Society; **118.** *Omena Resort*, [1903, Library of Michigan; **119.** Buehler Family Collection

All other illustrations are from author's collection.

Sources

Books and Pamphlets:
Holmes, Amanda J. *Omena a Place in Time: A Sesquicentennial History 1852-2002.* Omena, MI: Omena Historical Society, 2003.

Leelanau Township Historical Writers Group, *A History of Leelanau Township*. Chelsea, MI: Friends of Leelanau Township Library, 1982.

Mitchell, John C. *Wood Boats of Leelanau: A Photographic Journal.* Leland: Leelanau Historical Society, Leland, MI, 2007.

Omena Resort on Grand Traverse Bay, Omena Michigan, unknown author, unknown publisher, [1897]. Bentley Historical Library, University of Michigan.

Omena Resort, unknown author, Dickinson Bros., Grand Rapids, MI [1898]. Bentley Historical Library, University of Michigan.

Omena Resort, Omena, the "Beautiful" A.D. Greene, Dickinson Bros., Grand Rapids, MI [1901]. Bentley Historical Library, University of Michigan.

Omena Resort, Omena the "Beautiful," Unknown author Dickinson Bros., Grand Rapids, MI [1903], Library of Michigan, Rare Book Room.

Schopieray, Julie. *In So Distant a Place as Traverse City: the Northern Michigan Relatives of Elizabeth Bacon Custer*. Cedar, MI, Julie Schopieray, 2009.

Wakefield, Lawrence. *Sail and Rail: A Narrative History of Transportation in the Traverse City Region*. Grand Rapids, MI, Thunder Bay Press, 1980 & 1996.

Newspapers:
Detroit Free Press
Grand Rapids Herald
Grand Rapids Press
Leelanau Enterprise
Traverse City Record-Eagle

Periodicals:
Grand River Valley History. Vol 18, 2001.

Special Collections:
The Richmond Family Papers, Collection 94, Grand Rapids History Center, Grand Rapids Public Library
The Mary Richmond Kendall Photographs Collection, Collection 92, Grand Rapids History Center, Grand Rapids Public Library Beuhler Family Collection
Grand Rapids Archival Serials Collection, Collection 285

About the Editor

Christine Byron retired from her position as the Local Historical Collections librarian for the Grand Rapids Public Library in 2012. In her work, she became aware of the Richmond Family Papers Collection in the library's archives. The collection, donated by Miss Richmond, includes a variety of materials relating to the family including correspondence, writings, scrapbooks, ephemera, photographs, diaries and more. It is the diaries that drew Christine's interest, and is the subject of this book. It is a rare thing to have a first-hand accounts of cottage life in Leelanau County for the period she documented, 1907-1920. Her diaries give us a glimpse of that life and time, and Christine wanted to share that history with others.

Christine and her husband, Tom Wilson, have written five award-winning books in their "Vintage Views" series on Michigan history. Their sixth book, *Historic Leelanau: Recognized Sites and Places of Historical Significance* was a fundraiser for the Leelanau County Historic Preservation Society.

Christine serves on the board of the Michigan Postcard Club. She also is part of the planning committee for History Detectives, a program Christine started in 2008. Christine is a member of the selection committees for both the Michigan Notable Book Awards and the annual Michigan Author Award through the Library of Michigan.

Christine and Tom have received several awards, including the 2021 Volunteer of the Year Award from the Leelanau Historical Society for their work on the Michigan Historical Marker for the Clinton F. Woolsey Memorial Airport in Northport and their work on the Historic Leelanau book. In 2022 they received the Gordon Olson Award from the Kutsche Office of Local History at Grand Valley State University. And in 2025 they received the Baxter Award from the Grand Rapids Historical Society.

Christine and her husband have presented on a variety of historical topics for libraries, historical societies, and the Osher Lifelong Learning Institute at Aquinas College.